The implementation of IFRS in the UK, Italy and Ireland

by

Theresa Dunne
Suzanne Fifield
Gary Finningham
Alison Fox
Gwen Hannah
Christine Helliar
David Power

University of Dundee

Monica Veneziani
University of Brescia, Italy

Monica Veneziani contributed one third of this work, with particular reference to Italy

Published by

The Institute of Chartered Accountants of Scotland
CA House, 21 Haymarket Yards
Edinburgh EH12 5BH

First Published 2008
The Institute of Chartered Accountants of Scotland

ISBN 978-1-904574-23-1
EAN 9781904574231

This book is published for the Research Committee of
The Institute of Chartered Accountants of Scotland.
The views expressed in this report are those of the authors
and do not necessarily represent the views of
the Council of the Institute or the Research Committee.

No responsibility for loss occasioned to any person acting
or refraining from action as a result of any material
in this publication can be accepted by the authors or publisher.

Printed and bound in Great Britain
by T. J. International Ltd.

CONTENTS

FOREWORD

The move to International Financial Reporting Standards (IFRS) for many listed companies in Europe, and elsewhere, has been the biggest change to corporate financial reporting of recent times. The process has not been without problems but the ultimate aim of increased comparability and international harmonisation of financial reporting remains a necessity for international business. This is illustrated by the recent SEC announcement of a proposed roadmap, which would lead to the required use of IFRS by US issuers by 2014.

The impact, benefits and costs of the transition to IFRS were always expected to vary from country to country, with each country having its own starting point, characteristics and culture. This comparative study therefore investigates the implementation of IFRS in the UK, Italy, and Ireland.

The study examines: the resultant changes in financial reporting, in terms of the additional disclosures and the impact of IFRS on profit and equity; the costs involved in implementation of IFRS; the most problematic international accounting standards for adopters; and the usefulness of the resulting IFRS information from the perspective of preparers and users.

The report finds that the impact varied by country both in terms of the volume of disclosure and the impact on results. The biggest implementation problem related to the time commitment involved in the changeover and certain standards were identified as particularly problematic in this process. In terms of the usefulness of IFRS information, Italian interviewees were more positive than their UK and Irish counterparts on the changes introduced by the adoption of

IFRS. The report concludes with eight policy recommendations for consideration by users, preparers and regulators, including the IASB.

This project was funded by the Scottish Accountancy Trust for Education and Research (SATER). The Research Committee of The Institute of Chartered Accountants of Scotland (ICAS) has also been happy to support this project. The Committee recognises that the views expressed do not necessarily represent those of ICAS itself, but hopes that the report will aid companies which are implementing international standards at a later point, either as required by regulation or on a voluntary basis, and assist in the future development of international financial reporting.

David Spence
Convener, Research Committee
September 2008

ACKNOWLEDGEMENTS

We are grateful to Michelle Crickett and Angie Wilkie for all their help and work in putting together this monograph. We are also grateful to David Spence, David Wood and Isobel Sharp, as well as the Research Committee members for their support and advice. We would also like to thank all those who participated in the project by giving their time to us and allowing us to interview them.

Finally, the Research Committee and the researchers are grateful for the financial support of the Trustees of the Scottish Accountancy Trust for Education and Research; without this support the research would not have been possible.

EXECUTIVE SUMMARY

Introduction

In 2005 many companies in the EU were required to issue their financial statements based on International Financial Reporting Standards (IFRS) for the first time. A number of concerns had been raised about IFRS, some real and some serious. An independent assessment was, therefore, necessary to examine the implementation of IFRS and to assist future adopters of IFRS.

This study examines the implementation of IFRS in three countries: the UK, Italy and Ireland. The study focuses on these three countries because it was expected that companies in countries with a similar national accounting environment, such as the UK and Ireland, would experience similar reporting changes following the adoption of IFRS, and that companies in countries with a very different reporting environment, legal system and culture, such as Italy, would be affected differently by the adoption of IFRS. For example, the UK and Ireland are common law countries with accounting standards that focus primarily on the needs of shareholders, while Italy has a legal system based on civil law where traditionally creditors are viewed as being the most important users of financial statements. Thus, it was expected that the implementation of IFRS, with its shareholder focus, would require more of a cultural change in Italy than in the UK or Ireland.

The following research objectives are addressed in this study:

- To quantify the nature and extent of the changes in financial reporting that have been experienced as a result of IFRS adoption. In particular, the study examines the increase in disclosure relating to these new accounting standards as well as the changes to net profit and equity when comparing national Generally Accepted Accounting Practice (GAAP) to IFRS GAAP.

- To assess the costs associated with the production and publication of the new information.
- To identify the standards which have caused the greatest challenges for preparers and users to implement, reflecting education and training needs, changes to valuation models and the need for a general understanding of the accounting requirements and concepts.
- To examine the usefulness of IFRS information from the perspective of preparers and users of financial statements, both from the usefulness of the contents being mandated as well as the formats in which the additional information must be disclosed.
- To review whether the information required under IFRS decision-useful for stakeholder.

The above research objectives are considered within the framework of decision-usefulness to assess whether IFRS is more useful to users than national GAAP for making investment decisions, after consideration of the costs involved for both preparers and users.

Three different methods of analysis were used to examine the introduction of IFRS when addressing the above research aims:

- a content analysis of financial statements;
- an analysis of the reconciliation statement between IFRS and national GAAP; and
- interviews with multiple-stakeholders on the adoption of IFRS, including interviews with preparers, auditors, analysts and regulators.

Each of these three methods provides an international comparison on the adoption of IFRS between the UK, Italy and Ireland. While the results of each part of the project are reported separately, there emerges a comprehensive evaluation of whether the adoption of IFRS has been useful in each of the three countries. This approach contrasts with much of the extant literature which deals with specific issues or standards.

A content analysis of financial statements

The contents of 175 companies' financial statements were analysed: 138 UK companies; 27 Italian companies; and 10 Irish companies - reflecting the number of companies listed on each market. The findings from the content analysis comparison of company annual reports pre-IFRS and post-IFRS suggests that companies in Italy were more affected by the adoption of IFRS; the size of Italian annual reports grew far more significantly than those published in the UK or Ireland, although even in the latter two countries the annual reports increased substantially in length post-IFRS.

In Italy, on average, 73 pages of the post IFRS annual reports related to new information required by IFRS; this compared with just 13 pages in the UK documents and 19 pages in Ireland. This differential impact reflected the fact that the IFRS standards were a greater departure from Italian GAAP. Thus, many more pages of explanation were typically included regarding the transition to the new reporting regime. For example, 67 of the 73 pages of Italian annual report disclosure related to the implementation and impact of individual standards; this compared with 12 pages in the UK and 17 pages in Ireland where less explanation was typically required regarding the impact of individual accounting treatments.

IAS 32 Financial Instruments: Presentation, *IAS 39 Financial Instruments: Recognition and Measurement* and *IFRS 7 Financial Instruments: Disclosures* accounted for a large proportion of the extra disclosure. Overall, roughly one third of the extra disclosure related to financial instruments. In the UK and Ireland an extra four and six pages respectively were devoted to disclosures related to these three standards. In Italy the effect was even more pronounced with disclosure relating to the derivatives standards running to 32 pages. In the UK and Ireland the next most frequently discussed topic related to *IAS 19 Employee Benefits*, with about one page devoted to pension disclosure. In Italy this standard ranked third but the associated disclosure was still larger than that typically provided in the other two countries, covering three pages. The second biggest disclosure topic in Italy related to *IAS 14 Segment Reporting*. The area of segmental reporting was not covered by a specific accounting standard in Italy prior to the introduction of IFRS; thus, on average six additional pages of a typical Italian company's annual reports were used to comply with *IAS 14* requirements.

For the UK and Ireland, most of the extra disclosure was narrative rather than numerical in form; in the UK and Ireland respectively, 80% and 85% of the disclosures were narrative. This contrasts sharply with the situation in Italy, where most of the extra disclosure was numerical in nature; 55% of the annual reports were devoted to numerical summaries in Italy, much of this concentrating on the provision of information relating to derivatives and other financial instruments.

A breakdown by market listing and industry sector was analysed for the UK companies. This disaggregation revealed that FTSE 100 companies accounted for most of the disclosure, typically providing 16 pages of information; compared to other FTSE companies that typically presented half this level of disclosure. The sectoral analysis indicated that oil and gas as well as utility companies supplied more IFRS-related disclosure than other industrial groupings in the UK. A similar exercise could not be undertaken for the Italian and Irish Companies due to the composition and size of the samples.

Impact of IFRS on profit and equity

IFRS 1 First-time Adoption of International Financial Reporting Standards requires companies to produce a reconciliation of their IFRS equity and profit/loss to their equity and profit/loss reported under national GAAP. The sample was based on the financial statements used in the content analysis, although some companies were excluded because it was not possible to analyse their reconciliation statements.

Using these reconciliation statements an index of conservatism was calculated to assess the differences in profits and equity reported under IFRS as compared to that under national GAAP: what would national GAAP figures have been as a percentage of IFRS GAAP? The impact of IFRS on the reported profit and net equity of the sample companies is summarised in Tables 1 and 2 where the national GAAP profit or net equity figure is shown as a percentage of the IFRS net profit or net equity figure. As can be seen from Table 1, the implementation of IFRS increased the reported profit of companies in the UK, Italy and Ireland such that national GAAP profit was only 66%, 85% and 89% of the IFRS profit respectively.

Table 1 Net profit under national GAAP as a percentage of IFRS net profit - selected standards

	UK	Italy	Ireland
	%	%	%
Net profit	66	85	89
IFRS 2	100	101	101
IFRS 3	79	82	90
IAS 10	95	100	100
IAS 12	102	101	98
IAS 38	97	98	100
IAS 39	101	104	100
IAS 40	96	100	100

Notes:

The table is based on Table 4.4 in chapter four. Only those standards which have a sizeable impact on profit are included in the above summary table.

A percentage above 100% indicates that profit under national GAAP is higher than the profit under IFRS, ie profit has decreased due to the introduction of IFRS.

A percentage below 100% indicates that profit under national GAAP is lower than the profit under IFRS, ie profit has increased due to the introduction of IFRS.

It is also apparent from Table 1 that the standard that has the greatest positive impact on IFRS profit is *IFRS 3 Business Combinations* with the magnitude of this item as a percentage of the profit figure in national GAAP income statement being: 79% of its counterpart in the IFRS income statement for UK companies; 82% of its counterpart in the IFRS income statement for Italian companies; and 90% of its counterpart in the IFRS income statement for Irish companies. *IAS 10 Events after the Balance Sheet Date* (UK only), *IAS 38 Intangible Assets* (except Ireland) and *IAS 40 Investment Property* (UK only) also increased IFRS profit. Three standards had a negative impact on IFRS profit; *IAS 12 Income Taxes* (except Ireland), *IFRS 2 Share-based Payment* (except UK) and *IAS 39 Financial Instruments*, such that profit under national GAAP was higher, because of the impact of these standards. However, the effect on profit varied greatly across the sample companies; for example, the impact of *IAS 40* on national GAAP profit ranged from an increase of over 2,500% (a company in the UK) to a less than 1% decrease (a company in Italy).

By contrast, the net equity of the average company was less under IFRS, such that national GAAP net equity was higher by as much as 153% in the UK and 106% in Ireland but was slightly lower in Italy where national GAAP net equity was only 97% of IFRS equity (Table 2).

Table 2 Net equity under national GAAP as a percentage of IFRS net equity - selected standards

	UK	Italy	Ireland
	%	%	%
Net equity	153	97	106
IFRS 2	99	100	100
IFRS 3	96	97	98
IAS 10	87	100	96
IAS 12	104	99	107
IAS 16	99	99	100
IAS 19	167	102	104
IAS 32	100	101	100
IAS 38	99	99	100

Notes:

The table is based on Table 4.6 in chapter four. Only those standards which have a sizeable impact on equity are included in the above summary table.

A percentage above 100% indicates that equity under national GAAP is higher than equity under IFRS, ie equity has decreased due to the introduction of IFRS.

A percentage below 100% indicates that equity under national GAAP is lower than equity under IFRS, ie equity has increased due to the introduction of IFRS.

This reduction in IFRS net equity in the UK was mainly attributable to the effects of *IAS 19 Employee Benefits* where the national GAAP equity was 167% of the IFRS net equity, thus net equity under IFRS has reduced substantially as a result of the implementation of *IAS 19.* This standard also reduced net equity in Ireland. *IAS 12 Income Taxes* (except Italy) and *IAS 32 Financial Instruments: Presentation* (in Italy) also reduced the IFRS net equity. *IFRS 2 Share-based Payment, IFRS 3 Business Combinations, IAS 10 Events after the Balance Sheet Date, IAS 16 Property, Plant and Equipment*, and *IAS 38 Intangible Assets* impacted net equity favourably under IFRS; all five standards on average increased the IFRS reported net equity. However, the range of the impact of some of these standards was enormous; for example, the implementation of *IFRS 3* resulted in a decrease of almost 1,500% in net equity for one company in the UK while another company, in Italy, experienced an increase in net equity of 30% as a result of this standard.

Eleven accounting standards had no impact on the income statement or the balance sheet. These were:

IAS 7 *Cash Flow Statements;*
IAS 8 *Accounting Policies, Changes in Accounting Estimates and Errors;*
IAS 11 *Construction Contracts;*
IAS 14 *Segment Reporting;*
IAS 20 *Accounting for Government Grants and Disclosure of Government Assistance;*
IAS 24 *Related Party Disclosures;*
IAS 26 *Accounting and Reporting by Retirement Benefit Plans;*
IAS 29 *Financial Reporting in Hyperinflationary Economies;*
IAS 30 *Disclosure in the Financial Statements of Banks and Similar Financial Institutions;*
IAS 33 *Earnings Per Share;* and
IAS 34 *Interim Financial Reporting.*

These standards are all predominantly orientated to disclosure or focused on statements other than the balance sheet or income statement. Thus, most companies planning for the implementation of IFRS for the first time, could plan to focus their initial efforts on the other standards; it is unlikely that most companies will need to urgently embed any changes into their accounting systems regarding these standards as they do not affect the numbers reported to any significant extent. However, systems will be needed to collect any necessary information for disclosure purposes once the other standards have been dealt with.

Implementation costs and problems

From the 32 interviews that were conducted with various stakeholders, the biggest problem in all three countries when implementing IFRS related to the time commitment in getting up to speed on reading and understanding all the standards and assessing which ones would require the most work. A lot of time and money was spent on training staff and assimilating the new accounting requirements. This was particularly the case in Italy where a cultural change was required in order to shift from a creditor to a shareholder focus. Companies with multinational operations often held internal conferences where staff could get together for training sessions and receive feedback on implementation problems. Some standards were considered to be very technical in nature and required the assimilation of new and specific skills. This was especially the case for *IAS 39*, *IAS 19* and the impairment testing requirements of *IAS 36*. Often external consultants were engaged to provide the requisite skills that were not always available internally within companies. The interviewees identified that rules-based technical standards proved difficult to implement and monitor in practice. *IAS 39 Financial Instruments* is a key example as it adopts a more rules-based approach and as a consequence has resulted in many operational problems. However, the evidence from the interviews and reconciliation statement analysis shows that the implementation is more problematic than the impact on net profit or net equity.

In some companies, major changes were required to information systems, and different processes and operating modes were introduced to collect, process and disclose the extra information required under the new standards. This impact was particularly pronounced in banks and financial institutions. Overall, information systems had to be changed and planning was required in advance to adapt systems to cope with the new standards.

The language barrier created particular problems in Italy as all of the standards had to be translated from English into Italian and these translations were not always made available on a timely basis by the IASB. The availability of standards in all languages on a timely basis is essential requirement and an increase in the funding of the IASB may be necessary to produce these translations and to make them freely available on the IASB website. Indeed, the interpretation of standards across the many diverse cultures and languages that can exist within multinational organisations was a problem; internal conferences were often used by group companies to ensure that all their national offices possessed the same understanding of the key issues. There were also cultural differences evident in the accounting treatment choices that companies made in different countries. For example, in Italy, companies were more likely to choose the corridor approach available under *IAS 19* than their UK or Irish counterparts, partly because the latter countries were already familiar with a similar standard with no corridor approach *FRS 17 Retirement Benefits*.

Most companies relied heavily on their auditors to advise them on their IFRS implementation, especially in Italy, and in some industries the relevant trade bodies organised joint sessions for its members to debate the interpretation of certain standards. There was also a 'second mover' advantage in that companies with later year ends could review the financial statements of their peers or of best practice leaders to decide how to treat and disclose items that were a particular problem. Similarly, companies that have yet to implement IFRS can review the IFRS financial statements of companies that have already adopted IFRS and then decide how to deal with the requirements of certain standards.

The standards that caused the biggest problems in implementation were: *IAS 39*, *IAS 19*, *IAS 36*, *IAS 38*, *IAS 12*, *IAS 14*/*IFRS 8*, *IFRS 2* and *IFRS 3*. Most of this was because the accounting requirements were new and different and often required fair values, external data or key assumptions to be made to implement these standards. The planning process was also often hindered by the fact that the Big 4 audit firms did not always agree on the treatment of certain items. Some of the interviewees were annoyed that their auditor had taken a stricter view on the interpretation of some of the standards than the other Big 4 firms and that they had to spend a lot of time and money in numerous discussions with their auditors to get agreement on the treatment of these items. Further, some companies, especially the banks, thought that they were ahead of the Big 4 in their knowledge of certain standards, in particular *IAS 39*.

Interviewees thought that companies that do not need to produce IFRS statements are at a competitive advantage in some countries, such as Italy, because of the wider disclosure required by IFRS. With the increasing prevalence of private equity buyouts, many companies may be able to avoid more onerous reporting requirements.

Usefulness to users

The intention of the IASB has been to produce financial statements that are useful for decision-making. Rather than taking a narrower shareholder focus this study sought to examine their usefulness to a wider group of stakeholders. The study found that the impact on users in Italy was far greater than in the UK and Ireland. In Italy, analysts were more enthusiastic about the impact of IFRS and suggested that a common set of standards would facilitate comparability between companies and countries. In Italy, the users were very positive that IFRS now required financial statements to be aimed at investors and not creditors. For example, Italian GAAP does not require an earnings per share figure to be shown in the financial statements and the provision of this extra information via *IAS 33* was greeted favourably by the users. In Italy, the increase in disclosure was seen to be a positive feature of IFRS and there was better, clearer, classification of information under the new standards that enabled value-creation to be more clearly assessed. Further, fair values were considered to be more useful as forward-looking information that allowed the 'hidden value to emerge'. The reduced choice of accounting options from Italian GAAP also helped users compare financial statements and the increase in disclosure allowed the results of operations to be better evaluated because of *IAS 14*. The cultural shift in Italy was also helpful as, previously, Italian companies had often merely complied with the law and made disclosures in a limited way, but now the law had changed and they had to disclose far more information under IFRS.

UK and Irish interviewees were more cynical about the transition to IFRS and did not consider that the implementation of the new regime would alter or improve their analysis of companies' financial reports. They thought that IFRS-compliant annual reports were too complex and that users had to be financially literate to understand them. More specifically, the financial statements produced under IFRS had not changed any of their investment decisions and they did not consider them to be any more decision-useful than UK/Irish GAAP financial statements. UK and Irish users also complained that too much choice was allowed under IFRS compared to that which had previously existed under their national GAAP. Analysts thought that the mixed model of fair value and historical cost was very confusing and that the cash flow statement was the only meaningful report as it was the only one that had not been, as one interviewee noted: 'corrupted'. Preparers were unclear about whether the cost of implementation that had been incurred had outweighed the benefits as the costs were tangible and immediate but the benefits gained were intangible and longer-term.

Policy implications and recommendations

From the findings of this study, either in the content analysis, analysis of the reconciliation statement or the interviews, a number of policy implications are suggested as follows:

- From the findings of the interviews and content analysis, annual reports have increased in size and now typically include more complex information. It is suggested that shorter, simpler annual reports that highlight management performance and that can be used as a basis for assessing the future prospects of companies may be helpful and could perhaps be considered by regulators and the IASB.

- The interviews indicated that enhanced comparability of financial reports would be beneficial. The choices of accounting treatments, for example in *IAS 19 Employee Benefits*, needs to be limited so that the performance of global companies operating on an international basis can be assessed by all stakeholders. The IASB should therefore continue to work towards this objective by limiting choices within standards.

- From the analysis of the reconciliation statement data, the large reduction in net equity for UK companies may have implications for companies wishing to raise additional finance if the strength of their balance sheets has been eroded, with higher gearing levels and greater perceptions of risk. This may prove especially so with the recent credit crunch. Maybe companies should communicate openly with external parties and ensure that stakeholders understand that the financial strength of their operations has not been affected by the change in financial reporting standards *per se*, although the changes may bring to light an issue or a situation that has not previously been disclosed or recognised.

- The interviewees identified that, all users, not just expert users, need to begin to understand IFRS to ensure that they do not apply misleading valuations to company securities. Additional training should be undertaken by institutional investors and analysts.

- From the content analysis and interviews the effect of IFRS was far greater for Italian companies and Italian users than for those based in the UK and Ireland. Language and cultural issues were factors in this difference. Perhaps the IASB and EU should ensure that translations are made available in a timely manner across all jurisdictions and made freely available on the IASB website. Additional funding of the IASB may therefore be required to facilitate this.

- From the interviews, users need to engage more with the financial reporting process in order to understand and thus enhance the usability of financial reports and to ensure that published reports are useful for decision-making purposes. Perhaps more extensive communication and encouragement to engage in the IASB's consultation process would help in this regard.
- The interviewees also suggested that generic guidance should be produced to assist companies that are in the process of adopting IFRS about which standards to start with when planning the implementation of IFRS.
- From the interviews, it is suggested that audit firms and the professional bodies, such as ICAS, should be encouraged to produce joint documents advising on the interpretation and implementation of standards. Inconsistent advice between audit firms and belated advice have been confusing for preparers and users.

Summary

Overall, the implementation of IFRS has not been an easy process. Although the financial impact has often been negligible, the changes within organisations to their systems and processes should not be under-estimated. Hopefully these policy recommendations will be considered and progressed and that this will assist companies adopting IFRS in the future, so that they will find the process much easier.

1 Introduction

Introduction

One of the most fundamental changes to affect financial reporting in recent times has been the introduction of International Financial Reporting Standards (IFRS). Cairns (2004) describes these as:

> *The term 'IFRS' encompasses both IFRS issued by the IASB and international accounting standards (IAS) issued by the IASC and adopted or revised by the IASB.* (p.107)

This report uses the term IFRS in this manner to include all international accounting standards now in force (see Appendix F). These standards apply to the consolidated financial statements of EU listed companies for annual accounting periods beginning on or after 1st January 2005. Previous year comparatives also had to be shown in the first set of financial statements published under the new rules, together with reconciliations to the equity and profit figures that were calculated according to previous national accounting standards. Therefore, in the European Union (EU), the basis underpinning the preparation of the annual report as well as the components, formats and presentations of the financial statements changed dramatically. The current project examines a variety of aspects of these changes, and a detailed explanation is provided in the respective chapters.

Aims of the project

This project examines three issues associated with the introduction of IFRS in three separate strands: a content analysis of financial statements; an analysis of the reconciliation statement; and interviews with stakeholders on the adoption of IFRS (including the preparers' perspective on the adoption of IFRS). Each strand provides an international comparison on the adoption of IFRS between the UK, Italy and Ireland. The main research question that these strands address is whether the information required under the new IFRS is thought to be decision-useful for stakeholders. The different strands firstly quantify the nature and extent of the changes in financial reporting that have been experienced as a result of IFRS adoption and secondly consider the question of usefulness from the perspective of both the preparer and the user of the financial statements. In addition, the strands consider the usefulness of the contents being mandated as well as the formats in which the additional information must be disclosed. Further, the issue of usefulness is considered within the context of the costs associated with the production and publication of the new information. The costs to users in terms of training, changes to valuation models and understanding will also be discussed. While each strand of the project is reported separately, there emerges a comprehensive evaluation of whether the adoption IFRS has been useful. This approach contrasts with much of the extant literature which deals with specific issues or standards.

A content analysis of IFRS disclosures

The first strand of the research investigates the magnitude and the nature of disclosures provided by 175 UK, Italian and Irish companies in their pre-IFRS and post-IFRS annual reports and accounts, to facilitate an assessment of the impact of IFRS on the financial reporting practices of companies. Chapter three reports on the results of this exercise. This comparative analysis identifies the companiess that provided information on IFRS in their annual reports before the introduction of the new regime and provides a benchmark against which to judge the 2005 disclosures. Although this assessment is not generalisable in the sense of a market-based study, the data provides a very rich picture and a snapshot of early IFRS compliance.

An analysis of the reconciliation statements

This strand of the project obtains information about the nature of the monetary differences brought about by the move to IFRS. An examination of the reconciliation statement gives an insight into the impact of reporting under IFRS on both the net profit and the net equity of companies. Furthermore, it has been possible to identify the impact of individual standards on net profit and the net equity as a proportion of the total IFRS adjustment. This part of the project has gathered data on the magnitude of the IFRS changes, as well as the sources of any differences, whether in the income statement items or balance sheet figures. The results are reported in chapter four.

Interviews with stakeholders

The third part of this project reports on a consultation with a variety of financial reporting stakeholders, including finance directors, treasury and other company personnel, institutional investors, analysts and bankers from a mix of industries across different-sized companies in order to ensure that a range of perspectives is obtained. A semi-structured questionnaire instrument was employed to ensure that a common set of issues was raised with the interviewees. All interviews were taped and transcribed in full. The investigation assesses the impact on interviewees of the changes to the processes and the procedures involved in the preparation of annual reports associated with the introduction of IFRS. These findings are reported in chapters five and six. Chapter five ascertains how preparers, users and auditors have responded to the move towards IFRS including:

- planning for the change-over to IFRS;
- the operational changes that were required;
- the problem standards to implement; and
- the consultation process with stakeholders.

Chapter six details:

- a summary of the consultation process and the first AGMs after the introduction of IFRS;
- disclosure and corporate reputation;
- the costs of implementing IFRS;
- the benefits of IFRS; and
- comparability and harmonisation.

Summary

This report provides a comprehensive study of the implementation of IFRS in three European countries. The report is organised as follows. Chapter two is the literature review that examines the development of the financial reporting process over the last few decades, internationally and in the EU, and reports on the few studies that have also looked at the implementation of IFRS as well as the financial reporting environment that exists in the three countries that are the focus of this study; the UK,

Italy and Ireland. Chapter three is the content analysis of a sample of financial reports in the three countries. Chapter four reports on the reconciliation statements in the same annual reports to determine which IFRS had the most financial impact on income and equity. Chapters five and six highlight the findings from the interviews with preparers, users, auditors and regulators. Chapter seven concludes the report and highlights a number of policy implications.

2 LITERATURE REVIEW

Introduction

This chapter documents the UK, Italian and Irish financial reporting environment and reviews the extant literature on the historical development of the IASB, the adoption of IFRS, the suggested costs and benefits of IFRS adoption, problematic standards and the impact of IFRS on financial statements. The chapter then documents the decision-usefulness framework that is used to underpin the focus of this study.

UK, Italian and Irish background

A number of differences exist between the reporting environments faced by companies operating in the UK, Italy and Ireland. These variations help to explain the differential application of IFRS across the three jurisdictions. Table 2.1 summarises some of the major differences and this section expands on these and highlights the likely implications of these for the implementation of the new reporting regime.

Table 2.1 Summary of the UK, Irish & Italian reporting environment

Subject	UK	Italy	Ireland
Major Sources of Regulation	• Company law • Accounting standards • Stock exchange requirements • Financial Services Authority (FSA)	• Company law • Accounting standards • Stock exchange requirements	• Company law • Accounting standards • Stock exchange requirements • Office of the Director of Corporate Enforcement (ODCE)
Legal System	• Common law	• Civil law	• Common law
Main users of annual reports	• Investors	• Creditors	• Investors
Basis of accounting	• Accruals concept dominates	• Prudence concept dominates	• Accruals concept dominates
Economy and market structure	• Large open economy • Well-developed capital market	• Large economy • Small stock exchange	• Small open economy • Small but well-developed stock exchange

Note: this table provides a summary of the key differences in the reporting environment faced by listed companies operating in the UK, Italy and Ireland respectively prior to IFRS implementation.

The first key difference that exists across the three countries relates to the legal systems in place. The UK and Irish legal systems are based on common law, while the Italian system derives from Roman civil law[1]. Under a civil (or code) law system accounting tends to be heavily regulated and regulations are typically incorporated into national laws (La Porta *et al.*, 1998); these legal provisions govern, to varying degrees, the financial reporting process. In Italy, accounting standards contribute, together with the provisions of the civil code, to the preparation of financial statements, but only in a subservient role. In other words, these standards are not compulsory but they have an integrative and interpretative function with respect to the provisions of the law (Marchi, 2000). By contrast, common law develops on a case by case basis. Statute law exists but it tends to be less detailed and permits the exercise of judgement. This means that financial reporting tends to be less heavily regulated by statute, although legal opinion holds that compliance with accounting standards is necessary to satisfy the general requirements of the law. The accounting standard setting process therefore assumes a more prominent role in the UK and Ireland.

The second major difference relates to the variation in the nature of ownership and governance that exists across the three countries. In the UK and Ireland there is a reliance on equity finance. Thus, the interests of this investor class dominate, and financial reporting is typically geared towards meeting the needs of these users. In addition, within this environment, financial reporting has a role to play in ensuring transparency exists, which is a crucial factor necessary to ensure market efficiency (Meek and Saudagaran, 1990). By means of contrast, in Italy, companies with centralised and familial ownership prevail. Finance tends to be sourced primarily from banks and thus, creditors, as opposed to investors, are considered to be the main recipients of corporate financial statements. In this environment, the primary users are less interested in detailed financial statements (Salvioni, 1992) as they have direct access to detailed information regarding a company's performance.

The third major difference relates to the application of the fundamental accounting concepts. In the UK and Ireland the accruals concept is key, whilst in Italy the concept of prudence dominates. The dominant accruals-basis underpinning IFRS is thus likely to be more problematic for Italian companies that are used to conservatism in terms of recognition and measurement of accounting items.

The fourth major difference relates to the differing structures of the three economies. The UK is a large open economy with a very well-established capital market. In contrast the Italian economy, although large and developed, has a small stock exchange, while Ireland has a small open economy with a small but well-developed stock exchange. As at 31st December 2007, the Dublin market had a total domestic company capitalisation of $143,905m (with 60 listed companies comprising this total), while for Milan and the London the equivalent figures were $1,072,535m (301 companies) and $3,851,705m (2,588 companies) respectively (World Federation of Exchanges, 2008).

Finally, while the accounting environments faced by UK and Irish companies are very similar a couple of important differences do exist. First, as a member of the Consultative Committee of Accountancy Bodies (CCAB), the ICAI was involved in the UK standard setting process and resultant standards typically include a separate section detailing differences for application by companies operating in the Republic of Ireland. These differences are primarily related to variations in taxation. Second, the Company Law Enforcement Act 2001 was introduced in Ireland in 2003 to strengthen compliance with some aspects of company law where supervision had previously been lax. These new powers primarily focused on governance matters and saw the establishment of an Office of the Director of Corporate Enforcement (ODCE), a new multi-disciplinary agency aimed at enforcing company law and conducting any necessary investigations and prosecutions. Furthermore, the Companies (Auditing and Accounting) Act 2003 introduced the Directors' Compliance Statement (DCS) into the Irish corporate landscape. Under this legislation, directors of large companies are required to provide statements regarding their company's compliance with certain legal obligations. It may be that these additional requirements impact on the application of IFRS in Irish companies.

The historical development of the IASB

Due to the variety of national GAAP that has developed within individual countries, as outlined above, the financial statements of companies that have been compiled to meet the requirements of one particular jurisdiction often yield very different results from financial statements which have been produced to meet those of another. As a result, reconciliation statements of published accounts are required in some capital markets - especially the US (Street *et al.*, 2000; Haller, 2002). For example, Street *et al.* (2000) found that by the mid-1990s, adjustments to reconcile IAS with US GAAP were needed for an increasing number of items including: deferred tax; property, plant and equipment; capitalisation of borrowing costs; and goodwill. They noted that the difference in the profit figure reached 20% for a number of companies in 1996 and that certain adjustments were material. Therefore, over time, the costs of such reconciliations increased, and the benefits from harmonising the financial reporting requirements of different countries became more apparent. In addition, as the process of globalisation gathered pace, it was argued that the harmonisation of accounting standards would enable stakeholders anywhere in the world to use a set of financial statements without worrying about different accounting and disclosure treatments (Street and Shaughnessy, 1998). Further, companies with subsidiaries in different countries could produce financial statements according to a single set of accounting standards (Buchanan, 2003).

A main driving force behind the harmonisation process was the establishment of the International Accounting Standards Committee (IASC) in 1973. The IASC's *Framework for the Presentation and Preparation of Financial Statements* had the 'usefulness' of information for making decisions at its core. Since the foundation of the IASC, professional accountancy bodies from different countries have worked together on this Committee to obtain consensus about a common set of accounting rules. From 1973 until 2001, the IASC issued IASs which were agreed by a majority of its 10 member countries (Australia, Canada, France, Germany, Ireland, Japan, Mexico, Netherlands, the UK and the US) (ICAEW, 2006). This new international process did not, however, stop other influential bodies publishing harmonisation initiatives. For example, the EU's Fourth and Seventh Directives, which were issued in

1978 and 1983 respectively, were very influential in the harmonisation process, prescribing detailed formats of financial statements for the first time. However, the impetus towards harmonisation was slow as these Directives were adopted by EU member states on different dates; for example, Denmark and the UK adopted the Fourth Directive in 1981 whereas Austria did not adopt it until 1996 (Haller, 2002).

The G4+1, which comprised the IASC and four of the main standard setting bodies from the US, UK, Canada and Australia (with New Zealand), complemented the work of the IASC and achieved a measure of success in harmonising their accounting practices during the 1990's. This group was originally set up as a think tank based on producing transparent, capital-markets-based financial reports (Street, 2006). The G4+1 issued 12 discussion papers on matters such as recognition and measurement, financial instruments, hedge accounting, leases and share-based payments (Street and Shaughnessy, 1998) and it gradually evolved to become an 'embryonic' standard setter. In 1998 the IASC issued its first invitation to comment, on a draft standard about business combinations, and this was the start of a new era of accounting standard setting where complex decisions could be made (Street, 2006). Although, progress towards harmonisation on a wider scale continued to be slow, the process was boosted in 1987 when the IASC and the International Organization of Securities Commissions (IOSCO) joined forces to create a set of core IASs (Haller, 2002), although these standards were not finalised and recommended to members until 2000.

On 1st April 2001, the IASB replaced the IASC and adopted the pronouncements of its predecessor, including the international conceptual framework for accounting and its emphasis on decision usefulness. The IASB's membership was based on technical expertise and comprised 12 full-time and two part-time members. A liaison role was also created for the national standard setters of seven countries, consisting of the G4 (and NZ) plus France, Germany and Japan. The IASB also created the International Financial Reporting Interpretations Committee (IFRIC) to provide interpretations of standards when the committee feel that a standard was unclear (ICAS, 2006; Fearnley *et al.*, 2007).

In 2005, the objective of the IASB was revised to promote convergence and the constitution was amended to formally recognise a wide range of other parties and organisations, including the European Financial Reporting and Accounting Group (EFRAG) which is a private sector body that is comprised of users, preparers, the accounting profession and national standard setters (Cairns, 2004). The IASB's constitution also became more flexible with a 'comply or explain' focus introduced into its due process that mirrored corporate governance developments (Street, 2006). Sir David Tweedie, the first and current chair of the IASB, considered that a more uniform approach to standard setting would gain investor confidence and help multinationals achieve benefits in the preparation of their financial reports by using one approach to income measurement. Further, he argued that a company's cost of capital would be reduced as a result of applying IFRS because investors would be able to understand all companies' reporting rules. He also argued that investors who had previously perceived companies as being risky due to a lack of understanding of their accounting rules would become more attracted to them as investments in the future (Street, 2002).

The resulting combination of IAS and IFRS has generated 2,300 pages of regulatory text and created 2,000 disclosure requirements (Ernst & Young, 2006). This doubles the requirements that were in force in 2000 in the UK and quadruples the national GAAP of France (Ernst & Young, 2006). Indeed, Ernst & Young (2006) found that annual reports had increased in length by 20-30% with an average of 65 pages, with 37 further notes to the accounts taking up many more pages. PwC (2006d) found that the annual reports of insurance companies in particular had increased substantially, with many UK insurance companies' annual reports doubling in size. Even companies that had been previously reporting under IFRS, for example Swiss Life, saw a 50% increase in the size of its financial statements.

The adoption of IFRS

Although over 100 countries now use IFRS (KPMG, 2007), the adoption process has been sporadic and inconsistent applications between countries still exist. For example, the EU and Australia adopted IFRS during 2005, New Zealand during 2007, and Canada has committed to adopt IFRS by 2010. Since the formation of the IASC, a significant number of IASs and IFRSs have been issued. However, the level of non-compliance with these standards has been noteworthy. Street *et al.* (1999) reviewed the 1996 annual reports of a sample of 49 companies in 12 different countries selected from a total of 221 companies that claimed to comply with IAS at that time. They reported that the extent of the reports' compliance with IAS varied widely and suggested that:

> *...while these companies may appear anxious to seek the international investment status that comes with the adoption of IAS, they are not always willing to fulfil all of the requirements and obligations involved.* (p.46)

Several authors have noted that this lack of consistency in the application of IAS and IFRS often results in reported income being over-stated (Street and Gray, 2002; Prather-Kinsey and Meek, 2004). Even more worryingly, non-compliance often does not result in a qualified audit report (Street and Bryant, 2000; Street *et al.*, 2000). Further, the adoption of international standards does not necessarily result in uniformity across countries as cultural differences may influence the interpretation of the standards and lead to significant differences in reported amounts (Schultz and Lopez, 2001). For example, KPMG (2006) examined 26 IFRS options within 22 countries and found that the choices made were influenced by the previous national GAAP and that there was no cross border consistency between industries. For example, under *IAS 19 Employee Benefits* UK companies chose the equity method to reduce income volatility; whereas in Italy companies tended to use the corridor approach. Further, Ernst & Young (2006) found that format choices were determined on a country basis too; for example, UK companies tended to choose the functional approach in the income statement, showing cost of sales, distribution costs and administrative costs, while Italian companies chose to disclose the nature of costs such as purchases, employee costs and depreciation. PwC (2006d) also showed, in its study of 26 European insurance companies, that the choice of accounting policy was made based on whether the previous GAAP was Anglo-Saxon or not. For example, companies in Anglo-Saxon countries chose to put adjustments through the income statement whereas their counterparts in non-Anglo-Saxon countries opted to put adjustments through equity. Thus, the remaining influence of prior domestic standards resulted in similarities between companies in one country rather than between sectors across borders. For example, German pharmaceutical companies appear to bear more resemblance to German automobile companies than to French pharmaceutical companies (KPMG, 2007). Further, supplementary information is very diverse and, again, there appears to be a national bias (Ernst & Young, 2006).

Further, some EU countries which have the closest national GAAP to IFRS, for example the UK and Ireland, were not the first countries to adopt IFRS; the new EU member countries of Eastern Europe became the early adopters, possibly aiming to enhance their reputation within the EU (Sellhorn and Gornik-Tomaszewski, 2006).

The literature suggests that a variety of issues may impact upon the level of IFRS adoption. For example, Jaggi and Low (2000) outline various socio-political, legal and environmental factors that may have an influence on the financial disclosure provided by reporting entities in various countries. Delvaille *et al.* (2005) and McLeay (2006) note that financial reporting is influenced by: the development of the capital markets in a country; the role of finance; the influence of the state; the accounting profession; commercial law; and taxation. Further, national GAAP in Anglo-Saxon countries has mandatory disclosure and greater information content than that of non-Anglo-Saxon countries (Daske and Gebhardt, 2006). Bush (2005) notes that the US uses a regulatory model for financial reporting, but that the UK is more aligned with continental Europe in that it uses a civil model for companies, including those that are listed. Brown and Tarca (2005) consider the influence of various financial reporting regulatory bodies in different EU countries including stock exchanges, regulators of stock exchanges (as in Italy), review panels such as the Financial Reporting Review Panel in the UK, and government departments. Therefore, it would appear that the adoption of IFRS is influenced by a variety of complicated factors.

It is also worth noting that many EU companies have used IFRS or US GAAP voluntarily for several years (Taylor and Jones, 1999; Tarca, 2004). In fact, non-US multinational companies have often adopted US GAAP rather than their own national standards, especially when seeking a listing on the New York Stock Exchange (NYSE) (Tarca, 2004). Within certain countries, for example Germany, such a choice has been possible for several years and companies have been able to use their own national standards, IFRS or US GAAP. Alternatively, until 2005, Italian law (TUIF) required only that financial statements be produced in accordance with 'internationally recognised' accounting standards (Haller, 2002).

Companies often use non-national GAAP for a variety of reasons (Auer, 1996; Dumontier and Raffournier, 1998; Joshi and Ramadhan, 2002; Adb-Elsalam and Weetman, 2003; Cuijpers and Buijink, 2005; Pirinen, 2005; Richer and Sellhorn, 2005; Van Tendeloo and Vanstraelen, 2005; Daske, 2006). Evidence suggests that the voluntary use of IFRS depends upon a number of factors, such as whether a company is audited by one of the Big 4 or whether the company is registered in a particular country (Street and Gray, 2002). In addition, companies often adopt IFRS voluntarily in order to: enhance their exposure in foreign markets; improve customer recognition; secure foreign capital;

or reduce the political costs of transacting business abroad (El-Gazzar *et al.*, 1999). Empirical investigation indicates that IFRS tends to be used on a voluntary basis by larger companies that have foreign stock exchange listings and where the percentage of total revenue from outside the home country is sizeable (Tarca, 2004).

Different countries within Europe have conflicting rules about whether IFRS should be applied to a listed company's consolidated accounts alone or to both its individual accounts and the consolidated accounts. In the UK, companies are permitted to make that choice. However, in Italy, it is now mandatory that individual accounts comply with IFRS. Notably, the purpose of consolidated financial statements is different from that of individual accounts. Consolidated accounts reflect the objectives of the IASB's conceptual framework of being decision-useful whereas individual accounts are used for tax, distributable reserves, dividend payments and regulatory purposes (Jermakowicz and Gornik-Tomaszewski, 2006; PwC 2006a; Sellhorn and Gornik-Tomaszwski, 2006; PwC 2007).

Although the IASB's standards have been accepted by certain jurisdictions, such as the EU, a number of countries have still not signed up to use them. The US was one major economy that had not yet agreed to adopt IFRS; instead, it kept its own standards issued by the Financial Accounting Standards Board (FASB) (Zeff, 1999). However, the Securities and Exchange Commission (SEC), which oversees the FASB and is a key member of IOSCO, has been supportive of cooperation between the IASB and FASB to minimise differences between the different accounting rules (Street *et al.*, 2000). In 2002, the IASB and FASB signed a Memorandum of Understanding, the Norwalk Agreement (Street, 2006), which stated that both Boards would co-operate in the convergence of US GAAP and IFRS. Joint projects were set up by both Boards to look into matters such as business combinations and revenue recognition. In 2005 the SEC set out its 'Road Map to Convergence' in order to develop high quality standards and started the process to allow foreign companies to file IFRS financial statements without a reconciliation statement (Zeff, 2007); and in November 2005 it stated that it would reconsider its pension standard (Street, 2006, Zeff, 2007). In August 2008, the SEC announced steps that would lead to the required use of IFRS by US issuers by 2014. Consequently, significant progress towards the harmonisation of international accounting standards has been made. This suggests that many commentators and companies have identified potential benefits of IFRS adoption.

Suggested benefits of IFRS adoption

The literature shows that some putative benefits may arise from the adoption of international standards including: access to capital; enhancing cross-border listings; providing better investment opportunities; increasing transparency; comparability (Jermakowicz and Gornik-Tomaszewski, 2006); and the opportunity to review existing policies (PwC 2006a). The Institute of Chartered Accountants in England and Wales (ICAEW) (2006) claims that corporate reporting underpins the operation of efficient capital markets and Darenidou *et al.* (2006) argue that better transparency and disclosure help external actors to monitor the actions of managers, reducing information asymmetry and the risk of expropriation, thus, lowering the required risk premium and reducing the cost of capital. However, Daske and Gebhardt (2006) and Jermakowicz and Gornik-Tomaszewski, (2006) did not find a lower cost of capital resulted from IFRS application. Nevertheless, the latter found that the cost of switching to IFRS was lower for companies that had already had extensive prior disclosures. If the adoption of IFRS changes the cost of capital there may be repercussions on the capital structure of companies and an impact on debt covenants. If the gearing of companies increases, and the earnings become more volatile, there could be repercussions on covenants on corporate debt securities as these are based on accounting numbers (Jermakowicz and Gornik-Tomaszewski, 2006; Fearnley *et al.* 2007).

Costs and impediments to IFRS adoption

One of the major criticisms of IFRS has been that it will bring much more volatility into the income statement thus making it more difficult to judge a company's performance (Jermakowicz and Gornik-Tomaszewski, 2006; KPMG, 2007). For example, prior research has found that 85% of managers in FTSE 350 companies found it more difficult to explain their results since IFRS adoption (PwC, 2006a). This research was corroborated by Ernst & Young (2006), who noted that companies tended to use non-IFRS information in their announcements and presentations, and by PwC (2006d), who found that nearly all the insurance companies in its sample gave an alternative measure of profit, usually European Embedded Value (EEV).

Although some of the costs of implementing IFRS may be transitory, extra resources and an overhaul of IT systems will often be required (Darenidou *et al.*, 2006; Jermakowicz and Gornik-Tomaszewski, 2006). A survey of the FTSE 350 by PwC (2006a) found that most companies had to either hire extra staff or use subcontractors to implement IFRS, and that significant changes had to be made to computing and other information systems, and that there was no opportunity to parallel run or pilot these new systems. PwC also reported that companies implemented IFRS either by using their finance staff or by setting up a project team and that a third of companies had spent over £1m on external costs and a substantial amount on internal costs. Ernst & Young (2006) also cited the time constraints on implementation as a problem.

Multiple studies suggest that a number of other impediments to IFRS adoption also exist for preparers, such as the complexity of the standards and the corresponding lack of guidance (Larson and Street, 2004; Ernst & Young, 2006; Jermakowicz and Gornik-Tomaszewski, 2006; PwC, 2006a; Fearnley *et al.*, 2007; ICAS, 2007a;). For many preparers, the application of IFRS was the first time that they had applied complex accounting techniques, as in *IAS 19* (Larson and Street, 2004).

The translation of IFRS into local languages, such as Hungarian, and the time lag before these translations have become available to preparers has also proved problematic. For example, in Switzerland the translation time lag was over a year (Larson and Street, 2004; PwC, 2006a). Problems were also experienced by analysts when translating 'equivalent' financial reports into English to be able to make useful comparisons, making these reports less clear and less accessible (PwC, 2006d).

The absence of an IFRS that is equivalent to a national standard is problematic, for example, the UK's *FRS 5 Reporting the Substance of Transactions* (Fearnley and Hines, 2002). Further, many stakeholders consider that small companies should be excluded from the IFRS process, and that an IFRS equivalent to the UK ASB's *Financial Reporting Standard for Small Entities* (FRSSE) should be specially introduced for small companies (Fearnley and Hines, 2002). Indeed, many small companies consider IFRS too complicated to adopt (Larson and Street, 2004) but there is some support for the same GAAP being used by large and small companies (PwC, 2006a). The IASB did issue an exposure draft of an *International Financial Reporting Standard for Small and Medium-sized Entities* in 2007 and is currently considering the consultation responses.

A further problem was encountered when many preparers and auditors had to plan for IFRS before it had been fully agreed upon and adopted by the EU. *IAS 39 Financial Instruments: Recognition and Measurement* is a classic case, where, because of the (mainly French) banks, a 'carve out' was eventually agreed. Further, Ernst & Young (2006) note that as of 31st December 2005, only 12 months after the IFRS implementation date in the EU, there had already been amendments to two of the standards and four IFRIC interpretations. Nevertheless, most companies did not even refer to the new accounting treatment in their financial statements.

Some standards are also considered to be inconsistent with the conceptual framework and in conflict with other standards (Ernst &

Young, 2006). Sir David Tweedie (ICAS, 2007a) commented that *IAS 32* and *39* were: 'overly complex [and] inconsistent with the conceptual framework and or/each other' (p.9). This situation is further complicated by the fact that the conceptual frameworks of the UK ASB, the US FASB and the IASB are based on decision-usefulness whereas those of other countries often adopt a stewardship perspective (ICAS, 2007a; PAAinE, 2007).

Companies also tend to manage the markets by feeding analysts with information for them to put into their models. This often includes forward-looking information which may not be covered by accounting standards (KPMG, 2007); this might hinder the goal of convergence (Bush, 2005). The Conceptual Framework project of the IASB and FASB is focused on developing a common conceptual framework that is principles based to get around these problems (IASB, 2006).

As a result of these impediments to IFRS adoption, many have suggested that financial statements have become 'boiler-plate' reports with companies disclosing essentially the same sorts of information (ICAEW, 2006; KPMG, 2007) that technically comply with regulators' requirements (Ernst & Young, 2006). Thus, it is possible that financial statements are no longer serving the stated purpose of decision-usefulness (Ernst & Young, 2006). Consequently, some business and investment decisions may have been affected by the use of IFRS. For example, many companies have reviewed their pension plan provisions and others have gone as far as to close their defined benefit plans to new and even existing members because of the disclosure of large pension fund deficits (Jones and Cunningham, 2003).

IFRS has also affected the acquisition and merger decisions of a number of companies as well as the use of share-based payment schemes, especially in smaller companies (PwC 2006c). From a user perspective, IFRS has also affected investment decisions. There is evidence to suggest that some preparers are very negative about the impact of IFRS for users, although users themselves are much more positive. For example, PwC

(2005) show that, in its sample of companies, 29% of investors had disinvested because of IFRS and 21% had decided not to invest in a company in the first place. In this survey, some investors thought that IFRS accounts were useful in discerning operational and financial risks and 70% of users thought they were useful overall (PwC, 2005). These findings are very similar to a later PwC user study in seven European countries in 2006. Cross-country replies were very similar, apart from Italian users, where 96% agreed that IFRS were significant enough to change their perceptions about companies. Users believed that the IFRS changes had a significant impact on their perceptions of companies and on their investment decisions (Ernst & Young, 2006; PwC, 2005).

Problematic standards

Concerns have been raised about a decline in the quality of financial statements. Most of these concerns, within an EU context, have focused on *IAS 39 Financial Instruments: Recognition and Measurement*, especially for larger companies (PwC, 2006a) in the context of certain industries (PwC, 2006b; PwC 2006d; PwC, 2007). Other issues such as the lack of agreement about *IAS 39* (Fearnley and Hines, 2002) and the final EU carve out have also caused concern. IFRS adoption has required companies to account for, and disclose, their financial instruments, recognise derivatives on the balance sheet and/or use hedge accounting restrictions for the first time (Cairns, 2004). For example, Jermakowicz and Gornik-Tomaszewski (2006) found that financial instruments explained the biggest instance of new disclosure, with 41% of their sample companies reporting on financial instruments for the first time. They found that over half their sample companies had disclosed new information for the first time after adopting IFRS while over a third had multiple areas of new disclosure. Ernst & Young (2006), in a study of 65 of the largest companies in the FT Global 500 companies, noted that 9% of financial asset values and 6% of financial liabilities related to derivatives that were in the balance sheet for the first time.

The complexity of *IAS 39* is one of the major contributors to the claim that IFRS are complex. Michael Young, a New York lawyer, analysed the complexity of FAS 133, the US rules-based standard on financial instruments running to hundreds of pages, and contrasted it to the few pages of the Declaration of Independence which is very concise and based on principles. He commented that '…as an attorney I'd much rather be defending the Declaration of Independence' (ICAS, 2007b).

Another problematic standard is *IAS 19 Employee Benefits* (Fearnley and Hines, 2002; Cairns, 2004; KPMG, 2006; PwC, 2007) in terms of its complexity and its possible inpact on the income statement (Jermakowicz and Gornik-Tomaszewski, 2006; PwC, 2006a). Ernst & Young (2006) note that *IAS 19* and *IAS 37 Provisions, Contingent Liabilities and Contingent Assets* are two of the standards where companies do not comply with *IFRS 1 First-time Adoption of International Financial Reporting Standards* regarding their estimates of assumptions, such as mortality and the sensitivity of the numbers to the underlying assumptions.

A third standard that has been subject to comment in the literature is *IFRS 2 Share-based Payment* (Jermakowicz and Gornik-Tomaszewski, 2006; PwC, 2006a; PwC, 2007). Ernst & Young (2006) note that 90% of companies had charges to the income statement under this standard where previously there had been little disclosure. Smaller companies, such as those listed on AIM, appear to have been particularly affected (PwC, 2006c). Another standard that has caused a lot of controversy is *IFRS 3 Business Combinations* which allies itself to *IAS 36 Impairment of Assets* because of its impact on income statement volatility, particularly for certain industries (Jermakowicz and Gornik-Tomaszewski, 2006; PwC, 2006a; 2006b; 2007). Ernst & Young (2006) report that half of the companies in its sample reported impairment to goodwill while two thirds reported impairments to assets more generally.

IAS 12 Income Taxes and the associated change in deferred taxation is another standard that has caused problems (Fearnley and Hines, 2002; PwC 2006b), although KPMG (2006) found that FTSE 250 companies were more affected by deferred tax than the FTSE 100. Haverals (2007) examined the impact of *IAS 12* on Belgian companies and found that there was a sectoral bias with the automobile and construction industries recording the largest increases in their effective tax rates.

Other cited problem standards include *IAS 33 Earnings per Share*, *IAS 31 Interests in Joint Ventures*, *IAS 37 Provisions, Contingent Liabilities and Contingent Assets* and *IFRS 8 Operating Segments* (Jermakowicz and Gornik-Tomaszewski, 2006). The latter standard has particularly upset some users, mainly the Publish What You Pay coalition, with its focus on management reporting rather than geographical disclosure. The extent of the use of *IAS 17 Leases* and its associated problems have also come under the spotlight (ICAS, 2007b). Other notable standards include *IAS 16 Property, Plant and Equipment* (PwC, 2006b), *IAS 18 Revenue* (PwC, 2007), and *IFRS 5 Non-current Assets Held for Sale and Discontinued Operations*, which Jermakowicz and Gornik-Tomaszewski (2006) show was the cause of the second biggest increase in new disclosure from previous national GAAP. *IAS 38 Intangible Assets* has also appeared to cause concern (Fearnley and Hines, 2002; Jermakowicz and Gornik-Tomaszewski, 2006; PwC, 2006a; PwC, 2006b; PwC, 2007).

The impact of IFRS on the financial statements

A few studies have already analysed the impact of IFRS implementation on the financial statements of companies. In their study of Australian companies, Goodwin and Ahmed (2006) found that a move to IFRS from Australian GAAP had a bigger impact on larger companies. Over half of the smaller companies reported no change in their net income and, where there was a difference, it was generally an increase in net income and volatility that was due to *IAS 12 Income*

Taxes because of the deferred tax assets on tax losses. Most of the larger companies experienced a negative impact of IFRS in earnings because of the tax effect of asset write downs. Other important changes were found in the accounting requirements for *IFRS 2 Share-based Payment*. Smaller companies experienced changes in: goodwill, which resulted in an average increase to income and equity of 12%; *IAS 36 Impairment of Assets*; *IAS 38 Intangible Assets* including the treatment of research and development. *IAS 19 Employee Benefits*, *IAS 39 Financial Instruments: Recognition and Measurement* and *IAS 18 Revenue* all had a small negative impacts on earnings. On the balance sheet there was a small change in net assets, but liabilities tended to increase. Overall, compliance with IFRS had not been too onerous, and often there was a small positive impact. This result complements the findings of Jermakowicz and Gornik-Tomaszewski (2006) who noted that they also found a positive impact with net equity, rising by 11%.

Aisbitt (2006) found that, in the UK, although there was little overall effect of IFRS on FTSE 100 companies, the change in certain items could be significant. There was a sectoral bias with, for example, a negative impact of IFRS on health care equity but a positive impact on consumer goods and the one technology company in her sample. She found that there was no correlation between the level of disclosure and its impact on net equity. The standards that had the biggest effect on net equity, according to Aisbitt, were *IAS 19 Employee Benefits* which was associated with a negative 15% movement, and retirement assets with a 3% positive impact, *IAS 16 Property, Plant and Equipment* with a positive 11% impact, *IAS 7 Cash Flow Statements* with a positive 8%, *IAS 12 Income Taxes* that impacted the deferred tax assets and liabilities by 6%, *IFRS 3 Business Combinations* with a 4% decline and *IAS 39 Financial Instruments: Recognition and Measurement* with a 4% increase. Within these changes there were wide variations; goodwill had the highest standard deviation of 113% followed by *IAS 16* at 79%. The standards that were most commonly present in the IFRS reconciliation statement were *IAS 19 Employee Benefits*, *IFRS 2 Share-based Payment*, *IAS 10 Events after the Balance Sheet Date*, *IAS 18 Revenue*, *IAS 12 Income Taxes*, *IAS 16 Property, Plant and Equipment*, *IAS 32/29 Financial Instruments*, *IAS 21 The Effects of Changes in Foreign Exchange Rates* and *IAS 17 Leases*.

Aisbitt (2006) also found that the standards that caused the biggest financial impact were different from those standards that had caused the biggest problems in disclosure. Her analysis of the disclosures associated with IFRS showed that the standards relating to the disclosure of financial instruments was the most problematic, followed by disclosure on items such as pensions, goodwill, share-based payments, deferred taxation, impairment, dividends, intangibles and business combinations. The two standards that appeared to be problematic in both parts of her study (financial impact and disclosure), were *IAS 19* and *IAS 39*.

The ICAEW also published, in October 2007, its report for the European Commission on the EU implementation of IFRS. It also found that *IAS 39* had been a problem, together with the valuation of intangibles under *IFRS 3*. On average, it found that changes were required to accounting policies in seven areas: deferred taxation; pensions; financial instruments and derivatives; impairments; revenue recognition; goodwill, consolidations and intangibles; and employee share options. This study also found that boiler-plate disclosures were becoming more pronounced and that there were numerous occasions where companies either: did not disclose accounting policies or how they had applied them; or disclosed policies that were completely irrelevant to the companies.

Theoretical framework - decision-usefulness

The first half of this chapter has outlined the differing environments faced by companies in the UK, Ireland and Italy respectively and noted that the differing market and cultural characteristics across the three jurisdictions have resulted in varying degrees of emphasis on particular aspects of financial reporting. However, the over-riding criterion for the IASB in promulgating its programme of harmonisation has been the provision of useful information to decision-makers. This decision-usefulness framework is used as the theoretical lens for the present study; the remainder of this chapter will describe this framework.

In September 1989, the IASC published its *Framework for the Preparation and Presentation of Financial Statements*. This document was largely based on the equivalent document issued by the FASB in the US. However, it was not issued as an accounting standard and therefore does not over-ride individual IFRS. The IASC's framework was divided into seven major sections:

- the objectives of financial statements;
- underlying assumptions;
- qualitative characteristics of financial statements;
- the elements of financial statements;
- recognition of the elements of financial statements;
- measurement of the elements of financial statements; and
- concepts of capital maintenance.

In the first section the framework stated that the objective of financial statements was:

> *[To] provide information about the financial position, performance and changes in financial position of an enterprise that is useful to a wide range of users in making economic decisions.* (IASC, 1989, paras. 22 and 23)

It then discusses why users need to know about profitability, financial position, financial adaptability and cash generation. Similar discussions can be found in the frameworks of both the FASB and the UK's Accounting Standards Board (ASB)'s *Statement of Principles*. Decision-usefulness, therefore, provides a logical approach for the current investigation since it allows the research team to evaluate the financial statements produced under IFRS against an objective that the standard setting body has itself proposed.

Focusing on the effects of EU companies reporting under IFRS, this project adopts a decision-usefulness approach which 'stresses decision models and focuses on decision-makers' (Belkaoui, 2004, p.3). The notion that accounting systems should produce useful information for rational decision-makers is well-established within accounting research. As far back as 1955, Chambers pointed to 'the use of accounting statements as the basis for making decisions of practical consequence' (Chambers, 1955, p.17). He argued that 'the information yielded should be relevant to the kinds of decision the making of which it is expected to facilitate' (pp.21-22). Sterling (1972) also concentrated on the usefulness of information provided by financial statements. Indeed, he stressed the importance of usefulness over other criteria such as verifiability and objectivity, arguing that annual reports should 'supply information for rational [decisions] ... that are most likely to allow decision-makers to achieve their goals' (Sterling, 1972, p.198).

The assumption that annual reports should supply information which is useful for decision-making purposes has been readily accepted by accounting standard setters. For example, in the US, the FASB in Statements of Financial Accounting Concepts No.1 stated that:

> *Financial reporting should provide information that is useful to present and potential investors and creditors and other users in making rational investment, credit and similar decisions. The information should be comprehensible to those who have a reasonable understanding of business and economic activities and are willing to study the information with reasonable diligence.* (FASB, 1978, p.34)

This statement by US regulators was built on the view outlined by the Institute of Chartered Accountants in England and Wales (ICAEW) in *The Corporate Report* (ICAEW, 1975) which had, as its basic philosophy, the notion that financial statements should attempt to satisfy the information needs of users. This view was mirrored by the IASC's stance when it was established in 1973.

Researchers in the decision-usefulness tradition have typically consulted different groups who use financial statements to ascertain what information is used or considered to be useful. These researchers have employed questionnaires (Lee and Tweedie, 1979), observed users in decision-making settings (Carsberg and Day, 1984) examined the reports of users (Govindarajan, 1980) or studied equity returns to see if investors had impounded financial statement information into share prices (e.g. Beaver *et al.*, 1980). Most of these researchers have focused on the investor analyst group on the grounds that these are expert users, who can be easily consulted and whose advice is influential as a sizeable proportion of the (especially UK) stock market is owned by institutional investors (Mallin, 1999). This research approach has yielded insightful findings such as: the importance attached to information in the profit and loss account as well as the balance sheet (Arnold and Moizer, 1984); the lack of appetite amongst US and UK investors for inflation-adjusted financial statement numbers (Appleyard and Strong, 1984; De Berg and Shriver, 1987); and the desire among financial statement users for segmental disclosures (Collins, 1975; Balakrishnan *et al.*, 1990). Most recently, the approach has been employed by Beattie and Pratt (2001, 2003) in their analysis of web-based business reporting.

However, this decision-usefulness approach suffers from a number of criticisms. Problems with specifying which user groups to consider (Dey, 1999), how to handle conflicts between the needs of different users (Cyert and Ijiri, 1974), how to get users to convey their views on what information is needed (Carsberg and Day, 1984), as well as the trade-off between information usefulness and the cost of disclosure (Edwards and Smith, 1996), have all been documented.

The fundamental concept of the purpose of financial statements is a priority for the IASB and the FASB. Some commentators argue that financial statements should be for stewardship purposes and others argue that decision-usefulness is the key requirement. The IASB and FASB are, therefore, in the process of producing a new conceptual framework. This started with the Discussion Paper of July 2006 *Preliminary Views on an Improved Conceptual Framework for Financial Reporting* to:

> *...provide a sound foundation for developing future accounting standards and is essential to fulfilling the boards' goal of developing standards that are principles-based, internally consistent, internationally converged, and that lead to financial reporting that provides the information needed for investment, credit and similar decisions.*

Nevertheless, with such a fundamental change to the financial statements issued by companies that are now complying with IFRS, the emphasis on basic questions about the usefulness of information supplied seems appropriate. This study thus examines whether there are any differences in implementation between three European countries, namely the UK, Italy and Ireland to discover the changes in the quantity and type of disclosures and the impact that individual standards have had on the financial statements to discover if the standards are more decision-useful. Further, the implementation process that preparers, auditors, regulators and users have had to go through in order to adopt IFRS is examined to investigate whether users were at the forefront of preparers' minds or whether complying with IFRS was the over-riding objective.

Summary

This chapter has provided a brief overview of the accounting and financial reporting environment of the three surveyed countries – the UK, Italy and Ireland. A review of the literature has shown that the harmonisation of accounting standards is a process that started over 30 years ago and the consequent adoption of IFRS has been sporadic while its application remains somewhat inconsistent between countries. Prior research reports that many preparers have acknowledged a variety of costs and impediments to IFRS adoption. PwC (2006a) suggest that few preparers think that any internal value has been added, and that the new reports have neither hindered nor helped managerial decision-making, with the new regime being driven by political, and not commercial, considerations. This chapter has summarised the international standards that preparers have found most problematic and the impact that IFRS may have had on the financial statements of some companies. Overall, the message is mixed on the impact of IFRS. Finally, this chapter outlined the decision-usefulness framework that has been used as the focus of this study. This research project seeks to discover the impact of the implementation process of IFRS in three EU countries: the UK, Italy and Ireland and examines whether the financial reporting environment in these countries is now more decision-useful.

ENDNOTE

1 The common law system applies to the UK as a whole, however, Scotland also has a separate legal system which is based on Roman law. Business matters are regulated on a UK basis.

3 A Content Analysis of Annual Reports

Introduction

Chapter two outlined the background and context to the study. This chapter examines the impact that the 2005 introduction of IFRS visited on the annual reports and accounts of a sample of UK, Italian and Irish companies. In particular, a content analysis survey is used to explore changes in the magnitude and nature of IFRS-related disclosure evident in these documents prior to the reporting regime change (in 2004) and following the introduction of IFRS in 2005. The study conducts this analysis for the total level of IFRS-related disclosure, as well as for different categories of information. In addition, the analysis is performed for a wide variety of organisations, such that the findings should not be specific to any one market or industry sector.

The chapter commences with an overview of the content analysis research method. Details pertaining to the sample selection process are also provided. The specific application of the content analysis technique is then described. The empirical results are presented in aggregate; a breakdown is also given by variables such as market listing, industry sector and the nature of the information provided. The chapter concludes with a summary of the principal findings.

Content analysis

The first research method employed in this study is a form of content analysis. This method is used in order to collect data on the magnitude and nature of disclosures relating to IFRS implementation provided in a sample of UK, Italian and Irish annual reports. More details relating to the specific application of the technique in the present study are provided later in this chapter. However, this section provides a brief overview of the content analysis method and its appropriateness in the present study.

Krippendorff (1980) defined content analysis as

> *...a research technique for making replicable and valid inferences from data according to their context.* (p.21)

Thus, content analysis is a method of codifying the text (or content) of a piece of writing into various groups (or categories) depending on selected criteria (Weber, 1985). The implication is that a larger volume of disclosure for a particular category suggests that the category is important to preparers or readers of the text or document.

In order to act as an effective research tool, content analysis must encompass key characteristics; in particular, the process must be reliable and valid (Krippendorff, 1980; 2003). Reliability is one of the distinguishing characteristics of content analysis, in contrast to other techniques that are often used when describing or analysing the content of communication (Krippendorff, 2003). Krippendorff identified three types of reliability for content analysis: stability, reproducibility and accuracy. Stability refers to the ability of a judge to code data in the same manner over time (Milne and Adler, 1999; Krippendorff, 2003). The aim of reproducibility is to measure the extent to which coding is the same when multiple coders are involved (Krippendorff, 2003); in this context, intercoder reliability is the percentage of agreement between several coders processing the same textual material (Milne and Adler, 1999; Krippendorff, 2003). The accuracy measure of reliability involves assessing coding performance against a pre-determined standard, or against previous studies. There is a need for explicitly formulated rules and procedures to minimise the possibility that findings reflect the coders' subjective predispositions rather than the content of the documents under analysis (Krippendorff, 2003). Validity relates to how well the results of a study mirror reality (Jones and Shoemaker, 1994); in order to improve validity one needs to develop a coding scheme that guides coders in the analysis of content (Krippendorff, 2003). The coding scheme is an effort to make the coding process uniform across all coders so that the coding can be regarded as systematic (Krippendorff, 2003).

Within the present study, content analysis is viewed primarily as a qualitative research method, although the quantitative nature of the data collected in the process is recognised. It should be noted that, despite the technique's claims of objectivity, some subjectivity is inevitably involved in the choice of disclosure classification. However, the level of subjectivity is minimised through the development and pre-analysis of a rigorous set of decision rules.

The content analysis initially requires the selection of companies to be included in the investigation, while the second stage involves the development of an appropriate coding structure. The central part of the research can then take place, involving an investigation of the annual reports and the derivation of thematic variables; statistical analysis is used where appropriate to enable some explanation of the dataset.

Data and analysis

Content analysis has been used in numerous accounting and finance research studies (Jones and Shoemaker, 1994; Gray *et al.*, 1995; Dunne *et al.*, 2003). The present analysis draws on the work of previous content analysis studies, most notably on the framework developed by Gray *et al.* (1995) and Dunne *et al.* (2003). Choices have to be made in content analysis studies and this section summarises the reasoning behind the decisions taken when applying the technique in this research.

Sample

The aim of this strand of the research was to examine the introduction of IFRS on the financial reporting practices of a sample of companies adopting the regime in the UK, Italy and Ireland. This analysis focused on the non-financial statement sections of the annual reports. In other words, all of the annual report with the exception of the primary statements (Income Statement/Profit & Loss Account, Balance Sheet, Cash Flow Statement, Reconciliation Statement, Statement of Recognised Income & Expense/Statement of Total Recognised Gains & Losses) was included in the content analysis. The impact on the primary financial statements was analysed separately and the findings from this examination are reported in chapter four. In order to understand the impact of the new reporting regime the annual reports from a sample of UK, Italian and Irish companies pre- and post-IFRS implementation were analysed. Thus, the last reports produced under domestic GAAP were compared with the first produced under the international regime.

Table 3.1 Sample Details

	Total	UK	Italy	Ireland
Initial sample	211	171	30	10
Companies excluded:				
Data unavailable	14	14	0	0
Change in ownership status (mergers, de-listings, in administration, etc.)	16	15	1	0
2005 financial statements prepared under domestic/alternative GAAP	6	4	2	0
Final content analysis sample	175	138	27	10

In the UK, the FTSE 100 companies were examined. These companies represent the largest companies in the UK. In addition, a sample of 'other' FTSE listed companies was randomly selected to represent companies outside the largest grouping. The aim was to ascertain if the amount of disclosure provided by UK companies differed by company size. Of the initial UK sample of 171 companies, 33 companies had to be excluded for reasons set out in Table 3.1, resulting in a final sample of 138 (90 FTSE 100 companies and 48 'other' FTSE companies). The companies listed on the Milano Indice Borsa 30 (MIB 30) as of 31st December 2004 represented the initial group of companies chosen for the Italian investigation. The MIB 30 is a market capitalisation-weighted index of the thirty most capitalised and traded Blue Chip companies listed on the Borsa Italiana stock exchange in Italy[1]. The index had a base value of 10,000 as at 31st December 1992 and it is revised twice a year, typically in March and September, based on companies' liquidity and market capitalisation. In common with the UK sample, some companies had to be excluded (see Table 3.1). Ten Irish companies were randomly selected from the companies listed on the Irish Stock Exchange because, as of 31st December 2004, only 70 companies were listed on the Irish Stock Exchange, thus, ten companies were chosen to represent the disclosure practices of Irish companies. In the cases of Ireland and Italy there are fewer listed companies in existence, thus, a breakdown by size was of less relevance. All of these companies were included in the final analysis (Table 3.1). Thus, in total 175 pre-IFRS annual reports and 175 post-IFRS annual reports were analysed for this strand of the research. Basic information pertaining to the sample companies is provided in appendix A.

Pre-sample analysis

As discussed earlier in this chapter, pre-samples are typically employed in content analysis studies in order to develop the set of categories to be used in the analysis of the main sample (Krippendorff,

2003). These samples should ideally come from the same population as the main sample, so other annual reports were employed for this purpose. This pre-sample guided the development of the categorisation to be used in the content analysis. The detailed decision rules and template used for the content analysis are provided in appendices B and C respectively.

In any content analysis, decisions have to be made regarding the units of analysis to be used for the observation and collection of the data (Krippendorff, 1980; Gray *et al.*, 1995; Unerman, 2000). The annual report was used as the principal focus of the content analysis, primarily because accounting regulations, and IFRS in particular, are aimed at the accounting treatments and disclosures provided in this document, but also to reflect the fact that the annual report is usually viewed as the main form of corporate communication (Gray *et al.*, 1995; Adams and Harte, 1998). Therefore, the non-financial statement sections of the first annual report produced by each company after the introduction of the IFRS reporting regime, plus the last report issued under national GAAP, were used for this analysis[2]. As outlined in the detailed decision rules, the proportion of a page devoted to IFRS disclosure was used as the unit of analysis. Further, the percentage of the total annual report was also calculated. A clear standard A4 acetate grid[3], divided into one hundred boxes, was placed over the text to be analysed and the number of boxes containing IFRS-related text was recorded manually on the record sheet (see appendix C for an example of the record sheet used).

Gray *et al.* (1995) and Milne and Adler (1999) summarised the debate concerning the most suitable coding unit for content analysis; they concluded that the proportion of a page devoted to a particular topic was the preferred coding unit, as this measurement reflected the amount of space given to the issue and, by inference, the importance of that issue to the preparer of the document. This coding unit was therefore employed in the current study. It is recognised that there are difficulties associated with the use of the proportion of a page as the coding unit: for example, font size, margins, the use of graphics and partially blank pages that reports may contain can make coding more problematic (Tilt, 1997). However, the use of this measure takes into account information presented in tabular and graphic formats, which accounts for some of the IFRS information; it would be difficult to take account of such information if one chose to adopt words or sentences as potential coding units. Further, if the volume of disclosures is deemed to be an indication of the importance of a particular subject (Gray *et al.*, 1995; Unerman, 2000; Krippendorff, 2003), then it would seem inappropriate to exclude information presented in a form other than words and numbers.

Categories of disclosure

Prior to commencement of the content analysis of the sample companies' annual reports, a thorough review of the literature was undertaken (see chapter two). This process indicated a number of key issues of relevance for companies embarking on IFRS implementation, and resulted in the following categorisations:

- factual information;
- cost of implementation;
- general impact of implementation;
- progress to date;
- operational and strategic decisions taken by management;
- implementation and impact of individual standards; and
- general other.

These categories were chosen as the basic structure for the content analysis, as it was thought that companies would be most likely to discuss these core issues in their reports. An eighth category was added in order to capture the total IFRS-related information provided by the sampled organisations. A full set of decision rules relating to the categorisations used in the analysis is provided in appendix B.

Further classifications were undertaken based on the type of disclosure provided by the companies. The first additional classification concerned the narrative or numerical nature of such disclosures. The second concerned whether the disclosures were 'auditable'; if given access to the organisation, would it be possible to confirm a particular statement made in the reports. This assessment of auditability differs from the professional notion of audit but the classification has been used in previous content analysis studies (Gray *et al.*, 1995; Dunne *et al.*, 2003; 2004; Crawford *et al.*, 2007). Third, a 'news' categorisation was initially used to denote whether the reported information was good, bad or neutral in outlook for the organisation concerned. However, as the majority of the information reported turned out to comply with the standards, the 'auditable' and 'news' categorisations were considered less relevant and were thus excluded from the subsequent analysis. Finally, the location and page number of the disclosure within the annual report was noted; a memo field was also included to capture any additional information.

During the pre-analysis stage three researchers coded the sample documents. This process indicated that some refinement of the decision rules was necessary; in particular, adjustments were needed in order to categorise disclosures where an overlap of categories was found, or where a clarification of the coders' decisions was required. For example, during the pre-analysis stage it became evident that the information relating to particular topics was closely intertwined. This was particularly the case in relation to derivatives activities. *IAS 32 Financial Instruments*: *Disclosure and Presentation* details the disclosure requirements for companies with respect to their use of derivative financial instruments, while *IAS 39 Financial Instruments: Recognition and Measurement* contains measurement and valuation requirements. For the most part, particularly in the UK and Ireland, companies chose to provide the information required by these standards as one item; it was thus difficult to differentiate the information provided in this manner, and so it was decided to group this information together for the purposes of the content analysis. *IFRS 7 Financial Instruments: Disclosures* was released in August 2005 and also requires companies to discuss derivatives matters; although not effective until January 2007, some companies had adopted its provisions early, so this information was also included with the other derivatives-related disclosure. In a similar vein, the disclosures relating to goodwill activities were grouped together; goodwill is regulated under two standards, *IAS 38 Intangible Assets* and *IFRS 3 Business Combinations*, however, both of these standards also regulate other elements of the financial statements. Therefore, in this instance disclosures relating to goodwill were coded in an additional 'goodwill' category, while the remaining information required under *IAS 38* and *IFRS 3* was included in the appropriate category[4]. Companies also grouped their disclosures required by *IAS 28 Investments in Associates* together with their discussion of issues pertinent to *IAS 31 Interests in Joint Ventures*; where this amalgamation was evident, the disclosures were noted separately.

Following the pre-analysis, all of the main sample annual reports were coded according to the detailed decision rules devised in the earlier stage. The contents of the resulting record sheets were then transferred to an excel spreadsheet in order to permit subsequent analysis and to facilitate statistical manipulation of the data. This statistical analysis was conducted using Minitab software.

Results

The discussion of the results of the content analysis is divided into five sections:

- IFRS disclosure patterns by category evident in the total sample across the three countries;
- disclosure by market listing;
- disclosure by industry;
- by nature of disclosure; and
- a breakdown of the information provided by individual standard.

IFRS disclosure by category

Tables 3.2, 3.3 and 3.4 detail the level of IFRS-related information provided by companies in the UK, Italy and Ireland respectively across the seven disclosure categories outlined in the previous section. Panel A in each table presents this information based on the absolute number of pages of IFRS disclosure provided by the sampled companies, while Panel B documents the percentage of the annual report devoted to discussion of IFRS topics. All panels detail the level of disclosure prior to, and following, the introduction of the IFRS reporting regime, in addition to the difference in the quantity of disclosure, while the final column highlights the p-value. Specifically, where the p-value is <0.05, the difference is significant at the 95% level.

Table 3.2 UK sample – IFRS disclosure by category

Panel A – Number of pages of IFRS disclosure

Type of disclosure	Pre IFRS	Post IFRS	Difference	P-value
Factual information	0.3161	1.0009	0.6848	0.0000
Cost of implementation	0.0093	0.0164	0.0071	0.0320
General impact of implementation	0.1258	0.4097	0.2839	0.0000
Progress to date	0.0741	0.0264	-0.0477	0.0000
Operational & strategic decisions taken by management	0.0117	0.0067	-0.0050	0.5000
Implementation and impact of individual standards	1.2230	11.7080	10.4850	0.0000
General other	0.0000	0.0102	0.0641	-
Total	1.7600	13.1780	11.4180	0.0000

Panel B – Percentage of annual report devoted to IFRS disclosure

Type of disclosure	Pre IFRS	Post IFRS	Difference	P-value
Factual information	0.2802	0.8413	0.5611	0.0000
Cost of implementation	0.0065	0.0126	0.0061	0.0140
General impact of implementation	0.1137	0.2885	0.1748	0.0000
Progress to date	0.0764	0.0193	-0.0571	0.0000
Operational & strategic decisions taken by management	0.0091	0.0036	-0.0055	0.2570
Implementation and impact of individual standards	0.9730	8.6500	7.6770	0.0000
General other	0.0000	0.0058	0.0058	-
Total	1.4590	9.8220	8.3630	0.0000

Notes: This table shows the IFRS information provided by UK companies by disclosure category. Panel A presents this information based on the number of pages of IFRS-related information reported by companies across the seven disclosure categories. Panel B shows the percentage of the annual report devoted to IFRS-related information reported by companies across the seven disclosure categories. The mean p-values are based on a 2-sample t-test.

Table 3.3 Italy sample – IFRS disclosure by category

Panel A – Number of pages of IFRS disclosure

Type of disclosure	Pre IFRS	Post IFRS	Difference	P-Value
Factual information	0.8740	5.5240	4.6500	0.0000
Cost of implementation	0.1956	0.0000	-0.1956	-
General impact of implementation	0.2604	0.2107	-0.0496	0.6500
Progress to date	0.5119	0.0133	-0.4985	0.0000
Operational & strategic decisions taken by management	0.0074	0.0000	-0.0074	-
Implementation and impact of individual standards	1.4690	66.9000	65.4326	0.0000
General other	0.0463	0.1207	0.0744	0.2800
Total	3.3640	72.7700	69.4059	0.0000

Panel B – Percentage of annual report devoted to IFRS disclosure

Type of disclosure	Pre IFRS	Post IFRS	Difference	P-Value
Factual information	0.4514	2.3100	1.8582	0.0000
Cost of implementation	0.1091	0.0000	-0.1091	-
General impact of implementation	0.1371	0.0819	-0.0552	0.2200
Progress to date	0.2689	0.0050	-0.2638	0.0000
Operational & strategic decisions taken by management	0.0030	0.0000	-0.0030	-
Implementation and impact of individual standards	0.6890	27.3400	26.6499	0.0000
General other	0.0144	0.0593	0.0449	0.1270
Total	1.6730	29.8000	28.1219	0.0000

Notes: This table shows the IFRS information provided by Italian companies by disclosure category. Panel A presents this information based on the number of pages of IFRS-related information reported by companies across the seven disclosure categories. Panel B shows the percentage of the annual report devoted to IFRS-related information reported by companies across the seven disclosure categories. The mean p-values are based on a 2-sample t-test.

Table 3.4 Ireland sample – IFRS disclosure by category

Panel A – Number of pages of IFRS disclosure

Type of disclosure	Pre IFRS	Post IFRS	Difference	P-Value
Factual information	0.4420	1.3720	0.9300	0.0040
Cost of implementation	0.0080	0.0030	-0.0050	0.5700
General impact of implementation	0.1120	0.5220	0.4100	0.2320
Progress to date	0.0790	0.0090	0.0700	0.0040
Operational & strategic decisions taken by management	0.0000	0.0000	0.0000	-
Implementation and impact of individual standards	3.1500	16.7800	13.6300	0.0010
General other	0.0000	0.0000	0.0000	-
Total	3.7900	18.6900	14.9000	0.0010

Panel B – Percentage of annual report devoted to IFRS disclosure

Type of disclosure	Pre IFRS	Post IFRS	Difference	P-Value
Factual information	0.3930	1.0040	0.6110	0.0040
Cost of implementation	0.0049	0.0015	-0.0034	0.5230
General impact of implementation	0.0987	0.3360	0.2373	0.2650
Progress to date	0.0698	0.0080	-0.0618	0.0020
Operational & strategic decisions taken by management	0.0000	0.0000	0.0000	-
Implementation and impact of individual standards	2.3900	11.9800	9.5900	0.0000
General other	0.0000	0.0000	0.0000	-
Total	2.9600	13.3300	10.3700	0.0000

Notes: This table shows the IFRS information provided by Irish companies by disclosure category. Panel A presents this information based on the number of pages of IFRS-related information reported by companies across the seven disclosure categories. Panel B shows the percentage of the annual report devoted to IFRS-related information reported by companies across the seven disclosure categories. The mean p-values are based on a 2-sample t-test.

A number of points are worthy of note from these tables. First, the total amount of disclosure increased significantly with the implementation of IFRS. This observation is valid irrespective of the measure used. For example, Panel A of Table 3.2 reports that the mean number of pages of disclosure increased significantly from 1.76 pre-adoption to 13.178 post-IFRS implementation in the UK, while in Ireland a similar pattern is discernible with the mean percentage of Irish annual reports devoted to IFRS-related information rising from 2.96% to 13.33%. This evidence of substantial increases in overall levels of disclosure is not surprising given the introduction of the new reporting regime. Ernst and Young (2006) noted that the introduction of IFRS doubled the number of requirements in force across EU member countries, thereby, doubling the number of disclosures required in the UK and quadrupling the information required in France. The results of the present content analysis show that for the companies examined here the implications were even more profound with all three countries exhibiting increases in the number of pages devoted to disclosures in excess of that uncovered in the Ernst and Young study.

Second, and notwithstanding the consistent patterns of increases, differences are evident across the three countries surveyed. For example, Italy saw the most dramatic mean increase in both the number of pages and the percentage of annual reports discussing IFRS-related topics, from just three pages to 73 pages, while the UK recorded the least substantial, but still significant, changes. Previous research that was highlighted in chapter two has suggested that the transition to IFRS would be less problematic for particular EU countries, such as the UK and Ireland, that had domestic GAAPs that were more closely-aligned with their international counterparts prior to the transition (Sellhorn and Gornik-Tomaszewski, 2006). Furthermore, disclosure choices associated with differing interpretations of standards, and the options therein, across national boundaries (KPMG, 2006) might explain some of the variations noted, even after taking out the *IFRS 1* disclosures.

Third, while the total figures rose for all markets, irrespective of the measure used, this result masks some variation across disclosure categories. For example, disclosure relating to pre-implementation issues such as progress to date or operational and strategic decisions taken by management tended to decline in quantity following the regime change. On the other hand, disclosures relating to the implementation and impact of individual standards were large and significant, usually accounting for the bulk of the total increases reported in Tables 3.2, 3.3 and 3.4. For example, the mean number of pages of disclosure in Italy relating to the individual standards rose by more than 65, while the total rose by 69. This is in line with expectation, as most operational and strategic level planning would have been undertaken prior to the change in reporting. Further, the costs of implementing IFRS are viewed as being transitory in nature (Darenidou *et al.*, 2006; Jermakowicz and Gornik-Tomaszewski, 2006) so disclosure of these costs is likely to occur for one year only. Moreover, the substantial increases in the individual standard disclosures reflect the overall aim of the move towards IFRS in mandating reporting under a new set of standards.

Disclosure by market listing

For the UK data it was possible to undertake additional analysis across different markets. Disaggregation of this nature is common in content analysis studies, such as Dunne *et al.* (2003) and Crawford *et al.* (2007). The results of this analysis are displayed in Table 3.5. It was not possible to undertake a similar breakdown by market for companies listed in Italy and Ireland; all of the Italian companies are constituents of the MIB 30, while all of the Irish companies are listed on ISEQ.

Table 3.5 UK sample – analysis by market (number of pages of IFRS disclosure)

Panel A – FTSE 100

Type of disclosure	Pre IFRS	Post IFRS	Difference	P-Value
Factual information	0.4069	1.0536	0.6467	0.0000
Cost of implementation	0.0139	0.0200	0.0061	0.1820
General impact of implementation	0.1557	0.5226	0.3669	0.0000
Progress to date	0.0844	0.0339	-0.0505	0.0000
Operational & strategic decisions taken by management	0.0174	0.0099	-0.0075	0.5050
Implementation and impact of individual standards	1.6600	14.3300	12.6700	0.0000
General other	0.0000	0.0157	0.0157	-
Total	2.3390	15.9900	13.6510	0.0000

Panel B – FTSE other

Type of disclosure	Pre IFRS	Post IFRS	Difference	P-Value
Factual information	0.1458	0.9023	0.7565	0.0000
Cost of implementation	0.0008	0.0098	0.0090	0.0170
General impact of implementation	0.0698	0.1981	0.1283	0.0020
Progress to date	0.0548	0.0123	-0.0425	0.0010
Operational & strategic decisions taken by management	0.0008	0.0006	-0.0002	0.8420
Implementation and impact of individual standards	0.4017	6.7920	6.3903	0.0000
General other	0.0000	0.0002	0.0002	-
Total	0.6740	7.9150	7.2410	0.0000

Notes: This table shows the IFRS information provided by UK companies by market listing. This information is based on the number of pages of IFRS-related information reported by companies across the seven disclosure categories. Panel A presents this information for companies listed on the FTSE 100 market, while Panel B details this information for FTSE Other companies. The mean p-values are based on a 2-sample t-test.

Inspection of Table 3.5 reveals that the results reported earlier for the UK as a whole are robust to disaggregation by market. For example, the mean and median changes in total disclosure levels are positive and significant for both FTSE 100 and FTSE other listed companies. Again, the vast majority of this increase reflects the rise in disclosure relating to individual standards; the mean number of pages of disclosure in companies' annual reports rose by 12.67 for FTSE 100 companies and 6.39 for those in the FTSE other category. A similar analysis was undertaken based on the percentage of annual reports devoted to discussion of IFRS material; the results of this analysis are presented in appendix D (Table D.1). The findings reported in this appendix are entirely consistent with those presented in Table 3.5. Therefore, irrespective of whether disclosure is measured in absolute terms, using the number of pages, or relative terms, as a percentage of the annual report, the impact of the introduction of IFRS was both sizeable and statistically significant across companies in both UK markets.

Disclosure by industry

A breakdown by industry was also conducted for the UK sample. Similar analyses were not possible for Italy and Ireland as the sample numbers were too small and would not have generated meaningful results. The UK analysis by industry is provided in Table 3.6.

Table 3.6 UK sample – disclosure by industry

Panel A – Number of pages of IFRS disclosure

Industry	No.	Pre IFRS	Post IFRS	Difference	P-Value
Oil & Gas	4	2.0300	19.7100	17.6800	0.0200
Basic Materials	8	1.7080	14.9400	13.2320	0.0010
Industrials	25	0.8990	10.5380	9.6390	0.0000
Consumer Goods	15	3.5200	13.7400	10.2200	0.0000
Health Care	10	2.2370	11.7000	9.4630	0.0000
Consumer Services	32	1.4340	10.5250	9.0910	0.0000
Telecommunications	5	1.6080	13.8800	12.2720	0.0300
Utilities	8	3.5600	18.7100	15.1500	0.0010
Financials	26	1.4720	16.8800	15.4080	0.0000
Technology	5	0.5480	7.7800	7.2320	0.0090

Panel B – Percentage of annual report devoted to IFRS disclosure

Industry	No.	Pre IFRS	Post IFRS	Difference	P-Value
Oil & Gas	4	1.2240	11.5900	10.3660	0.0140
Basic Materials	8	1.2040	8.8600	7.6560	0.0000
Industrials	25	1.0510	9.7480	8.6970	0.0000
Consumer Goods	15	2.7360	10.3870	7.6510	0.0000
Health Care	10	1.8450	9.0300	7.1850	0.0000
Consumer Services	32	1.3630	9.3810	8.0180	0.0000
Telecommunications	5	1.1400	10.8500	9.7100	0.0010
Utilities	8	2.2110	12.5870	10.3760	0.0000
Financials	26	1.1390	9.3070	8.1680	0.0000
Technology	5	0.8810	10.2440	9.3630	0.0000

Notes: This table shows the IFRS information provided by UK companies by industry. Panel A presents this information based on the number of pages of IFRS-related information reported by companies across the seven disclosure categories, while Panel B displays the relative measure based on the percentage of annual reports devoted to such information. The mean p-values are based on a 2-sample t-test. The industry grouping is based on the Industry Classification Benchmark system (ICB). The No. column is the number of sample companies in each industry grouping.

The results shown in Table 3.6 illustrate that the evidence of significant increases in disclosure levels following the introduction of IFRS reported earlier is pervasive across all industry sectors. In particular, both the mean number of pages and percentage of annual report increase significantly in each of the ten industries. Perhaps surprisingly, given the effects of *IAS 32/39* relating to derivatives, the highest increases are not recorded in the financial industry for either measure of disclosure. PwC (2006d) noted the substantial increase in the size of annual reports produced by UK insurance companies; this increase was, in part, attributed to the enhanced requirements in reporting risk management. However, the findings of the present analysis, suggest that companies in the financial sector are not the only ones to have expanded this element of their reporting.

Nature of disclosure

Tables 3.7, 3.8 and 3.9 disaggregate the data according to the nature of the disclosure about IFRS in the non-financial sections of the annual reports of the sample companies. In other words, they show whether or not this IFRS disclosure takes a narrative or numerical form, for the UK, Italy and Ireland respectively.

Table 3.7 UK sample – narrative versus numerical disclosure

Panel A – Narrative number of pages of IFRS disclosure

Type of disclosure	Pre IFRS	Post IFRS	Difference	P-Value
Factual information	0.3137	1.0009	0.6872	0.0000
Cost of implementation	0.0080	0.0048	-0.0032	0.2300
General impact of implementation	0.0806	0.1684	0.0878	0.0000
Progress to date	0.0743	0.0264	-0.0479	0.0000
Operational & strategic decisions taken by management	0.0117	0.0062	-0.0055	0.4630
Implementation and impact of individual standards	1.0760	9.3040	8.2280	0.0000
General other	0.0005	0.0058	0.0053	0.0340
Total	1.5640	10.5170	8.9530	0.0000

Panel B – Numerical number of pages of IFRS disclosure

Type of disclosure	Pre IFRS	Post IFRS	Difference	P-Value
Factual information	0.0024	0.0000	-0.0024	-
Cost of implementation	0.0023	0.0116	0.0093	0.0000
General impact of implementation	0.0449	0.2413	0.1964	0.0000
Progress to date	0.0000	0.0000	0.0000	-
Operational & strategic decisions taken by management	0.0000	0.0004	0.0004	-
Implementation and impact of individual standards	0.1466	2.4280	2.2814	0.0000
General other	0.0000	0.0043	0.0043	-
Total	0.1962	2.6860	2.4898	0.0000

Notes: This table presents the results of the disaggregation of the IFRS information provided by UK companies by the nature of the information included, for example, whether the disclosure is numerical or narrative in form. This information is based on the number of pages of IFRS-related information reported by companies across the seven disclosure categories. Panel A presents details of the narrative content, while Panel B outlines the numerical content. The mean p-values are based on a 2-sample t-test.

Table 3.8 Italy sample – narrative versus numerical disclosure

Panel A – Narrative number of pages of IFRS disclosure

Type of disclosure	Pre IFRS	Post IFRS	Difference	P-Value
Factual information	0.8740	5.5240	4.6500	0.0000
Cost of implementation	0.1359	0.0000	-0.1359	-
General impact of implementation	0.2111	0.0148	-0.1963	0.0000
Progress to date	0.5119	0.0133	-0.4986	0.0000
Operational & strategic decisions taken by management	0.0033	0.0000	0.0000	-
Implementation and impact of individual standards	1.2910	26.9700	25.6790	0.0000
General Other	0.0463	0.0767	0.0304	0.5940
Total	3.0740	32.6000	29.5260	0.0000

Panel B – Numerical number of pages of IFRS disclosure

Type of disclosure	Pre IFRS	Post IFRS	Difference	P-Value
Factual information	0.0000	0.0000	0.0000	-
Cost of implementation	0.0596	0.0000	-0.0596	-
General impact of implementation	0.0493	0.1959	0.1466	0.1340
Progress to date	0.0000	0.0000	0.0000	-
Operational & strategic decisions taken by management	0.0041	0.0000	-0.0041	-
Implementation and impact of individual standards	0.1770	39.9300	39.7530	0.0000
General Other	0.0000	0.0441	0.0441	-
Total	0.2900	40.1700	39.8800	0.0000

Notes: This table presents the results of the disaggregation of the IFRS information provided by Italian companies by the nature of the information included, for example, whether the disclosure is numerical or narrative in form. This information is based on the number of pages of IFRS-related information reported by companies across the seven disclosure categories. Panel A presents details of the narrative content, while Panel B outlines the numerical content. The mean p-values are based on a 2-sample t-test.

Table 3.9 Ireland sample – narrative versus numerical disclosure

Panel A – Narrative number of pages of IFRS disclosure

Type of disclosure	Pre IFRS	Post IFRS	Difference	P-Value
Factual information	0.4420	1.3720	0.9300	0.0040
Cost of implementation	0.0060	0.0010	-0.0050	0.4320
General impact of implementation	0.0820	0.1320	0.0500	0.4790
Progress to date	0.0790	0.0090	-0.0700	0.0040
Operational & strategic decisions taken by management	0.0000	0.0000	0.0000	-
Implementation and impact of individual standards	2.7500	14.3800	11.6300	0.0000
General Other	0.0000	0.0000	0.0000	0.0010
Total	3.3600	15.8900	12.5300	0.0010

Panel B – Numerical number of pages of IFRS disclosure

Type of disclosure	Pre IFRS	Post IFRS	Difference	P-Value
Factual information	0.0000	0.0000	0.0000	-
Cost of implementation	0.0020	0.0020	0.0000	1.0000
General impact of implementation	0.0300	0.3900	0.3600	0.2710
Progress to date	0.0000	0.0000	0.0000	-
Operational & strategic decisions taken by management	0.0000	0.0000	0.0000	-
Implementation and impact of individual standards	0.4040	2.4020	1.9980	0.0260
General Other	0.0000	0.0000	0.0000	-
Total	0.4360	2.7940	2.3580	0.0270

Notes: This table presents the results of the disaggregation of the IFRS information provided by Irish companies by the nature of the information included, for example, whether the disclosure is numerical or narrative in form. This information is based on the number of pages of IFRS-related information reported by companies across the seven disclosure categories. Panel A presents details of the narrative content, while Panel B outlines the numerical content. The mean p-values are based on a 2-sample t-test.

The evidence presented in Tables 3.7, 3.8 and 3.9 suggests that, for the UK and Ireland, the biggest absolute increase in disclosure levels is observed within the narrative information supplied in annual reports. For example, in Ireland, the mean number of pages of narrative disclosure rises from 3.36 to 15.89, whereas the equivalent change in numerical information is from 0.43 to 2.79. However, for Italy, the largest absolute and proportionate rises occur in the case of numerical disclosure. Most of the increases in narrative disclosure related to the implementation and impact of individual standards classification while the provision of factual information ranked a distant second. With the increase in numerical disclosure, the implementation and impact of individual standards is again the largest category although general impact of implementation is now rated second. A similar analysis was conducted using the percentage of annual report devoted to IFRS information; this exercise produced similar results and this information is provided in appendix D (Tables D.2, D.3 and D.4).

Disclosure by standard

From the preceding analysis, it is evident that the disclosure category which experiences the largest increase in information provided in post-IFRS annual reports is the implementation and impact of individual standards classification. Detail relating to the information provided under each of the international standards was also gathered during the content analysis exercise.

Table 3.10 provides details about the number of pages of disclosure made regarding the implementation and impact of individual standards. Table 3.10 provides this information for the UK, Italy and Ireland respectively. A similar breakdown by standard was conducted using the percentage of annual report devoted to IFRS disclosures. This analysis produced similar results and confirmed that irrespective of whether disclosure was measured in absolute terms (using the number of pages) or in relative terms (as a percentage of the total annual report), the impact of the switch to IFRS on individual standards was pronounced. Appendix D (Table D.5) provides further details of this analysis.

Table 3.10 Disclosure by standard (number of pages of IFRS disclosure)

Standard	UK		
	Pre IFRS	Post IFRS	Diff
IAS 1	0.0250	0.1970	0.1720*
IAS 2	0.0060	0.0970	0.0910*
IAS 7	0.0060	0.1250	0.1190*
IAS 8	0.0020	0.0030	0.0010
IAS 10	0.0370	0.1580	0.1210*
IAS 11	0.0010	0.0220	0.0210*
IAS 12	0.0980	0.7150	0.6170*
IAS 14	0.0110	0.1440	0.1330*
IAS 16	0.0380	0.4530	0.4150*
IAS 17	0.0260	0.2770	0.2510*
IAS 18	0.0240	0.3490	0.3250*
IAS 19	0.1370	1.2270	1.0900*
IAS 20	0.0000	0.0140	0.0140*
IAS 21	0.0380	0.4240	0.3860*
IAS 23	0.0020	0.0420	0.0400*
IAS 24	0.0000	0.0780	0.0780
IAS 26	0.0000	0.0000	0.0000
IAS 27	0.0300	0.2900	0.2600*
IAS 28	0.0110	0.0770	0.0660*
IAS 29	0.0010	0.0010	0.0000
IAS 30	0.0000	0.0000	0.0000
IAS 31	0.0170	0.0840	0.0670*
IAS 33	0.0130	0.0560	0.0430*
IAS 34	0.0000	0.0000	0.0000
IAS 36	0.1270	0.3030	0.1760*
IAS 37	0.0140	0.2920	0.2780*
IAS 38	0.0570	0.4570	0.4000*
IAS 40	0.0040	0.0590	0.0550*
IAS 41	0.0050	0.0120	0.0070
IFRS 1	0.0260	0.1960	0.1700*
IFRS 2	0.1230	0.5790	0.4560*
IFRS 3	0.0420	0.3090	0.2670*
IFRS 4	0.0320	0.2690	0.2370*
IFRS 5	0.0080	0.1670	0.1590*
IFRS 6	0.0010	0.0340	0.0330*
*IAS 28/*31	0.0120	0.0820	0.0700*
IAS 32/39/IFRS 7	0.3040	3.7370	3.4330*
Goodwill	0.0560	0.3420	0.2860*

Note: The mean p-values are based on a 2-sample t-test. The significant results (at 95%) are indicated by an *

Table 3.10 Disclosure by standard (number of pages of IFRS disclosure) (cont.)

Standard	Italy		
	Pre IFRS	Post IFRS	Diff
IAS 1	0.0270	0.3340	0.3070*
IAS 2	0.0020	0.2520	0.2500
IAS 7	0.0020	0.3490	0.3470*
IAS 8	0.0000	0.0050	0.0050
IAS 10	0.0000	0.0000	0.0000
IAS 11	0.0000	0.0260	0.0260
IAS 12	0.0140	2.5800	2.5660*
IAS 14	0.0060	6.1800	6.1740*
IAS 16	0.0460	0.7560	0.7100*
IAS 17	0.0910	0.6430	0.5520*
IAS 18	0.0390	0.4350	0.4060*
IAS 19	0.0960	3.0810	2.9850*
IAS 20	0.0000	0.0850	0.0850
IAS 21	0.0070	0.5910	0.5840*
IAS 23	0.0040	0.4700	0.4660*
IAS 24	0.0240	2.2660	2.2420*
IAS 26	0.0000	0.4820	0.4820
IAS 27	0.0780	1.7500	1.6720*
IAS 28	0.0060	1.0430	1.0370*
IAS 29	0.0000	0.0040	0.0040
IAS 30	0.0000	0.0000	0.0000
IAS 31	0.0130	0.6410	0.6280*
IAS 33	0.0390	0.6240	0.5850*
IAS 34	0.0000	0.0000	0.0000
IAS 36	0.1030	1.4750	1.3720*
IAS 37	0.0770	2.2560	2.1780*
IAS 38	0.0660	0.6960	0.6300*
IAS 40	0.0020	0.2930	0.2910
IAS 41	0.0000	0.0000	0.0000
IFRS 1	0.2020	0.8100	0.6080*
IFRS 2	0.0380	2.7730	2.7350*
IFRS 3	0.0340	1.8120	1.7780*
IFRS 4	0.0070	1.3750	1.3670
IFRS 5	0.1150	1.0020	0.8870*
IFRS 6	0.0050	0.0430	0.0380
IAS 28/31	0.0000	0.0000	0.0000
IAS 32/39/IFRS 7	0.3270	32.0000	31.6730*
Goodwill	0.0000	0.0000	0.0000

Note: The mean p-values are based on a 2-sample t-test. The significant results (at 95%) are indicated by an *

Table 3.10 Disclosure by standard (number of pages of IFRS disclosure) (cont.)

Standard	Ireland		
	Pre IFRS	Post IFRS	Diff
IAS 1	0.0540	0.1210	0.0670
IAS 2	0.0110	0.1200	0.1090*
IAS 7	0.0000	0.0960	0.0960
IAS 8	0.0000	0.0000	0.0000
IAS 10	0.0590	0.1900	0.1310*
IAS 11	0.0000	0.0390	0.0390
IAS 12	0.3090	0.8260	0.5170
IAS 14	0.0500	0.0950	0.0400
IAS 16	0.0740	0.6490	0.5750*
IAS 17	0.0620	0.2540	0.1920
IAS 18	0.0350	0.9300	0.8950
IAS 19	0.3430	1.4060	1.0630*
IAS 20	0.0080	0.0750	0.0670
IAS 21	0.1250	0.7050	0.5800*
IAS 23	0.0000	0.0470	0.0470
IAS 24	0.0000	0.2100	0.2100
IAS 26	0.0000	0.0000	0.0000
IAS 27	0.0820	0.3910	0.3090*
IAS 28	0.0260	0.2130	0.1870
IAS 29	0.0000	0.0000	0.0000
IAS 30	0.0000	0.0000	0.0000
IAS 31	0.0040	0.1230	0.1190
IAS 33	0.0770	0.0320	-0.0450
IAS 34	0.0000	0.0000	0.0000
IAS 36	0.0390	0.3030	0.2640*
IAS 37	0.0000	0.3450	0.3450
IAS 38	0.1940	0.5280	0.3340
IAS 40	0.0000	0.0090	0.0090
IAS 41	0.0000	0.0000	0.0000
IFRS 1	0.0400	0.2200	0.1800*
IFRS 2	0.1810	0.8470	0.6660
IFRS 3	0.2300	0.3560	0.1260
IFRS 4	0.0120	0.2670	0.2550
IFRS 5	0.0000	0.1190	0.1190
IFRS 6	0.0000	0.0100	0.0100
*IAS 28/*31	0.0860	0.1690	0.0830
IAS 32/39/IFRS 7	0.9650	6.2900	5.3250*
Goodwill	0.0850	0.6460	0.5610*

Note: The mean p-values are based on a 2-sample t-test. The significant results (at 95%) are indicated by an *

Table 3.10 illustrates that, in each of the countries studied, there were significant rises in the amount of disclosure relating to most of the standards listed; for example, in the UK, 31 out of 38 mean differences were significant, as illustrated by the associated p-values. However, there was some variation in the absolute amounts of extra disclosure recorded; in particular, the number of pages relating to the *IAS 32/39/ IFRS 7* group of derivatives standards was the highest recorded for each of the three countries. This finding supports the conclusions of Aisbitt (2006) who found that *IAS 39* was the most problematic standard with regard to implementation and those of Jermakowicz and Gornik-Tomaszewski (2006) who stated that disclosures relating to derivatives activities reflected 41% of new disclosures provided by companies in the post-IFRS era.

In the UK and Ireland, the second highest increases related to *IAS 19 Employee Benefits*, with mean recorded rises of 1.090 and 1.063 pages respectively. *IAS 19* has consistently been highlighted as being, in addition to the derivatives standards mentioned above, one of the most problematic standards for companies complying with IFRS (Fearnley and Hines, 2002; Cairns, 2004; Jermakowicz and Gornik-Tomaszewski, 2006; KPMG, 2006; PwC, 2007). It is worth noting that, for companies in the UK and Ireland not adopting IFRS, a similar increase in disclosure for employee benefits would have been expected under national GAAP, with the implementation of *FRS 17 Retirement Benefits*. However, for Italy, although a large mean in pensions-related disclosure is shown in the table, the increases in disclosure relating to *IAS 14 Segment Reporting* were higher, registering a mean of 6.174. In the UK and Ireland, following IFRS implementation, *IAS 32/39/IFRS 7* and *IAS 19* were the only cases where more than a page in companies' annual reports was devoted to the new international standards. In Italy, however, there were 13 categories where the disclosure was now greater than a page in length.

Summary

This chapter has examined the disclosures made by 175 companies across the UK, Italy and Ireland before and after the introduction of IFRS in January 2005. The results indicate that the introduction of IFRS was associated with a large increase in internationally-oriented disclosures provided in corporate annual reports in each of the three jurisdictions. This observation holds irrespective of whether the actual number of pages of IFRS-related information disclosed, or the relative measure of the percentage of the annual report containing IFRS information, is used. The nature of the variation post-IFRS differs from standard to standard and across the three countries, but the implementation of IFRS has had a significant impact on the nature and magnitude of the information provided in corporate annual reports. The additional disclosure may have provided stakeholders with additional useful information about these companies. The perceptions of users, preparers and regulators regarding the impact of IFRS on the annual reports and their decision-making processes are discussed in chapters five and six. Prior to this, chapter four reports on the financial impact of the standards on the income statement and net equity.

ENDNOTES

1 The Borsa Italiana was acquired by the London Stock Exchange in October 2007.

2 This facilitated a comparison between the reports pre- and post-IFRS adoption, in order to evaluate the magnitude and order of the differences in company reporting following the introduction of the new regime. It is recognised that the use of the year leading up to and the year immediately following the introduction of IFRS does not take into account early adopters of the regime. This is a limitation of the current analysis. The present work could be extended by looking at early adopters of IFRS for a few years prior to their implementation.

3 A standard A4 margin was used in the template.

4 Except in Italy where companies primarily provide goodwill information under *IFRS 3*.

4 An Analysis of IFRS Reconciliation Statements

Introduction

IFRS 1 First-time Adoption of International Financial Reporting Standards requires companies to produce a reconciliation of their equity and profit/loss reported under national GAAP to their IFRS equity and profit/loss. This chapter examines the impact on profit and equity of reporting under IFRS for the first time and identifies the individual IFRSs that account for most of this impact. If no sizeable differences in profit and equity under the different accounting regimes are found, then any impact of the IFRS-compliant annual reports may simply be due to the new disclosure formats. However, if sizeable differences are being reported, it ought to be possible to identify the international standards that are responsible for these changes.

The remainder of the chapter is organised as follows: the second section details the sample used for the analysis of IFRS disclosures for all three countries – the UK, Italy and Ireland - while the third and fourth sections report the results. In particular, the third section presents an analysis of the percentage IFRS adjustments to profits and equity for all three countries together, while the fourth section reports the results from calculating an index of conservatism for total equity, total profit and each individual adjustment for all three countries separately. The final section presents a number of concluding observations.

Sample

Initially, the sample was based on those companies that had already been selected for the content analysis that was reported in chapter three. Table 4.1 shows that, after a number of exclusions, the sample consisted of 138 companies from the UK, 27 companies from Italy and 10 companies from Ireland; thus, data for 175 companies in total were analysed. Although *IFRS 1* requires reconciliations to be produced in such a way as to allow users to understand any material adjustments, it does not prescribe a specific layout. Consequently, a variety of presentations were encountered during an inspection of the annual financial statements of the sample companies and a further six companies were excluded because it was not possible to analyse their reconciliation statements. For example, one company reconciled its equity and profit to IFRS on a Modified Statutory Solvency basis instead of UK GAAP and another produced US GAAP reconciliations only.

Table 4.1 Sample details for the reconciliation statement analysis

	UK	Italy	Ireland	Total
Sample for analysis	138	27	10	175
Companies excluded as the reconciliation statement could not be analysed	6	0	0	6
Sample for analysis	132	27	10	169
Sub-sample analysed for the income statement	88	27	7	122
Sub-sample analysed for the balance sheet	92	27	6	125

Notes: This table outlines the sample of companies included in the analysis for this chapter. The financial statements had a variety of year ends throughout the year.

IFRS 1 specifically required first-time adopters to: (a) reconcile their equity reported under national GAAP to their equity under IFRS, both at the date of transition to IFRS and for the comparative period; and (b) reconcile their most recent annual profit/loss reported under national GAAP to the equivalent IFRS profit/loss. It also required first-time adopters to provide an explanation of any material adjustments to the cash flow statement but only where one had been presented under national GAAP. Given that not all companies would have produced a cash flow statement under national GAAP, this part of the reconciliation was excluded from the analysis. Although the standard does not prescribe a format for the reconciliation statement, the implementation guidance does contain an example of a line by line reconciliation of the financial statements. Bonham *et al.* (2004) suggest that such a presentation may be appropriate where a significant number of line items in the primary financial statements are affected by transitional adjustments. Alternatively, they propose that:

> *A straightforward reconciliation of the equity and profit or loss figures may be able to provide an equally effective explanation of how the adoption of IFRS affects the reported financial position, financial performance and cash flow.* (p.279)

As companies presented a variety of reconciliation statement formats, it was not always possible to attribute transitional adjustments to particular international standards. Of the 169 companies that produced a comprehensive reconciliation, only a sub-set provided information that allowed the researchers to attribute the transitional adjustments to specific IFRSs: further companies were therefore omitted from the investigation because the absence of a line-by-line reconciliation did not allow the impact of individual standards to be examined. The final sample for the income statement therefore consisted of 122 companies – 88 from the UK, 27 from Italy and 7 from Ireland. The final sample for the balance sheet included data for 125 companies - 92 from the UK, 27 from Italy and 6 from Ireland.

Analysis of IFRS disclosures

For the examination of the IFRS disclosures made by the final sample of companies in their reconciliation statements, the reconciliations are grouped according to the relevant standard and the amount of the adjustment expressed as a percentage of the total profit (loss) or total equity calculated in accordance with companies' national GAAP. These percentages are then analysed statistically and descriptive information produced. This information is produced for the whole sample and is presented in Tables 4.2 and 4.3. Table 4.2 shows income statement adjustments while Table 4.3 presents summary statistics on the balance sheet equity adjustments for all three countries.

Tables 4.2 and 4.3 are each split into eight columns; the first outlines the accounting standard associated with the IFRS adjustment while the next seven columns supply descriptive statistics. In particular, the mean percentage size of each adjustment, along with its standard deviation (SD), is provided. In addition, the median percentage size of the adjustment is also supplied in case the mean value is influenced by outlier observations. The minimum and maximum percentage size of the adjustment associated with each standard across all the companies in the sample is displayed in order to provide some insight into the range of adjustments made by the sample companies. Finally, two measures of the distributions of the adjustment percentages are given to test whether the data is normally distributed; skewness (Skew) measures the symmetry of the values around the mean while the kurtosis (Kurt) statistics indicate whether the distributions have bigger tails of more extreme observations than might normally be expected. If these statistics indicate that the distributions of the data is not normal, then care needs to be taken when examining the mean percentages; the median may provide a much better estimate of the adjustment for the typical company in the sample.

Table 4.2 Descriptive statistics of the IFRS income statement adjustments

	Mean	SD	Median	Min	Max	Skew	Kurt
Total profit per national GAAP	100.00	0.00	100.00	100.00	100.00	N/A	N/A
IFRS 2	-0.23	32.08	-0.69	-124.32	292.22	6.41	65.95
IFRS 3	29.73	85.57	3.47	-67.47	727.03	5.70	41.29
IFRS 4	0.77	5.47	0.00	-0.70	42.17	7.29	52.41
IFRS 5	0.34	2.80	0.00	-1.82	27.27	8.78	81.12
IAS 1	0.44	3.59	0.00	-0.65	35.00	8.82	81.60
IAS 10	7.45	54.03	0.00	-0.28	532.35	8.82	83.40
IAS 12	-9.51	66.09	0.00	-627.09	34.38	-8.20	72.88
IAS 16	-0.31	1.78	0.00	-13.33	3.42	-5.20	31.99
IAS 17	-4.14	42.30	0.00	-431.82	87.50	-9.50	97.52
IAS 18	-0.16	1.63	0.00	-12.50	3.19	-6.64	47.55
IAS 19	-1.61	12.12	0.00	-72.73	41.27	-3.07	17.26
IAS 21	-2.09	17.41	0.00	-180.28	6.21	-9.97	102.43
IAS 28	0.28	3.34	0.00	-3.11	34.87	10.30	107.84
IAS 31	1.19	15.87	0.00	-62.16	131.82	5.18	46.30
IAS 32	-0.16	1.54	0.00	-16.22	0.00	-10.47	110.06
IAS 36	-0.21	3.44	0.00	-32.43	13.82	-7.07	73.77
IAS 38	6.50	51.38	0.00	-45.45	494.75	8.47	77.42
IAS 39	-1.37	6.73	0.00	-51.99	19.76	-4.84	33.09
IAS 40	38.72	268.91	0.00	-0.13	2,506.70	8.16	69.96
IAS 41	0.83	8.79	0.00	-0.72	92.60	10.53	110.98
IAS 32/IAS 39	10.75	112.05	0.00	-10.34	1,180.17	10.52	110.81
IAS 27, 28 & 31	0.83	8.23	0.00	0.00	86.70	10.51	110.56
Goodwill	0.94	7.00	0.00	-35.47	40.11	1.62	19.58
IFRS 3 & *IAS 38*	1.05	6.52	0.00	0.00	49.51	6.42	41.57
Other	0.05	9.73	0.00	-43.78	61.42	1.36	18.94
Minority interests	-0.13	0.98	0.00	-7.61	1.81	-6.47	44.90
Reallocations	0.83	8.78	0.00	0.00	92.48	10.54	111.00
Total profit - IFRS	148.51	307.76	106.67	-340.91	2,963.41	7.36	65.27

Notes: Mean is the average, SD is the standard deviation, Median is the mid-point while Min and Max are the minimum and maximum values. A measure of skewness (Skew) and kurtosis (Kurt) are also given. In calculating these summary statistics, the absolute value of any loss was used in the denominator of the percentage change calculation.

Table 4.2 reports the impact of IFRS on the total profit (loss) calculated according to national GAAP, as at 31st December 2004 reported as a percentage of the national GAAP profit or loss. The reconciliation adjustments for IFRS are stated as a percentage of the absolute value of the total profit (loss) under national GAAP and reported for different standards. The percentages were calculated for each standard but those where the mean was zero, or very close to zero, are not reported separately in Tables 4.2 and 4.3 but included in the 'other' category to allow the reader to focus on those standards which gave rise to sizeable adjustments for this sample of companies. A very distinctive picture emerges from Table 4.2. On average, the impact of the reconciliation to IFRS has been to increase total profit by 48.51%. The main causes of this mean increase were *IAS 40 Investment Property* (38.72%), *IFRS 3 Business Combinations* (29.73%), *IAS 32 Financial Instruments: Disclosure and Presentation/IAS 39 Financial Instruments: Recognition and Measurement* (10.75%), *IAS 10 Events after the Balance Sheet Date* (7.45%) and *IAS 38 Intangible Assets* (6.5%). The impact of these adjustments on total profit under national GAAP was offset to some extent by changes required under *IAS 12 Income Taxes* (-9.51%), *IAS 17 Leases* (-4.14%) and *IAS 21 The Effects of Changes in Foreign Exchange Rates* (-2.09%) but the overall effect was an increase in total profit under IFRS.

The standard deviation values in Table 4.2 are sizeable for some of the accounting standards, indicating that there was considerable variation in their impact on the sample of companies. For example: *IAS 40 Investment Property* (268.91%); *IAS 32 Financial Instruments: Disclosure and Presentation/IAS 39 Financial Instruments: Recognition and Measurement* (112.05%); *IFRS 3 Business Combinations* (85.57%); *IAS 12 Income Taxes* (66.09%); *IAS 10 Events after the Balance Sheet Date* (54.03%); *IAS 38 Intangible Assets* (51.38%); and *IAS 17 Leases* (42.30%). This view is confirmed by the minimum and maximum values which are very large in a number of cases. For example, the range of adjustments for *IAS 40 Investment Property* varies from -0.13% to +2,506.70% of the total profit (loss) reported under national GAAP. Not surprisingly, the company where the adjustment for *IAS 40* was 2,506.70% of their total profit reported under national GAAP was Land Securities, the largest real estate trust in the UK. The adjustment of £897.4m helped transform a loss of £35.8m under national GAAP into a sizeable profit according to IFRS. Finally, it is worth pointing out that the distributions of the data are not normal and an analysis of Table 4.2 indicates that the median impact of the IFRS adjustments is to increase (reduce) total profit (loss) by 6.67%.

Some standards have affected the way the gains or losses on the revaluation of assets are accounted for while others have prohibited a particular accounting treatment that was permitted under national GAAP. For example, Bonham *et al.* (2004) argue that, in relation to investment properties:

> *[IAS 40] represents a major conceptual shift, as it is the first international standard to introduce the possibility of applying a full fair value model when accounting for non-financial assets. Under this option the asset is not depreciated, and all valuation changes (i.e. fair value changes) from one period to the next are treated as gains and losses and are reported in the income statement.* (p.693)

Under UK, Italian and Irish GAAP, these unrealised gains on investment properties would not have been disclosed in the income statement but would have been reported as a gain in the revaluation reserve. More specifically, under Italian GAAP, investment property companies only revalued their assets before IFRS when extraordinary events occurred. Given that the application of *IAS 40* has increased national GAAP profit it is safe to assume that most companies have experienced revaluation gains on their investment properties.

Likewise, under *IAS 32* and *IAS 39*, financial instruments must now be measured using a mixed-attribute model. This means that a financial instrument will rarely be accounted for based on its pure historical cost or on a pure fair value basis. Such an approach is different to the one previously adopted in the UK, Italy and Ireland. Also, any valuation gains or losses that flow through the income statement are likely to be, to some extent, dependent on the performance of the equity markets. By contrast, *IFRS 3* is likely to have resulted in a profit figure which was higher than that reported under national GAAP, due to its prohibition of goodwill amortisation that was previously permitted under UK as well as Irish GAAP and that was compulsory under Italian GAAP.

The reasons why *IAS 10* and *IAS 38* have had such an effect on profit are less clear. The *IAS 10* definition of events after the post balance sheet date is deliberately broad and therefore any increase in national GAAP profit following the application of *IAS 10* is likely to be due to circumstances that are relevant to individual companies as opposed to a change in accounting method. However, Bonham *et al.* (2004) explain that certain adjustments will be required on the initial application of *IAS 10* when the company has:

> *...more up to date information relating to conditions that existed at earlier balance sheet dates than it had when earlier financial statements were prepared.* (p.1873)

Similarly, the reason why *IAS 38* has resulted in a profit figure which was higher than that reported under national GAAP is not easy to explain. *IAS 38* permits the use of two alternative measurement concepts for intangible assets: the cost model and the revaluation model and requires those assets with a finite useful life to be amortised. It is therefore more difficult to attribute the increase in national GAAP profit to any one particular factor within *IAS 38* as not all companies will have applied the same measurement concept to their intangible assets and any differences are likely to be due to the choices available within the standard itself. However, in Italy, many listed companies are using the cost model for intangible assets (Teodori, 2006), thus the impact of *IAS 38* is most likely to be due to the joint effect of capitalising certain development costs (previously reported in the income statement) and prohibiting the capitalisation of start-up costs, research, and advertising costs (previously included in the balance sheet). Under Italian GAAP, companies can choose whether or not, under certain conditions, to capitalise these kinds of costs. Further, the impact may also be due to the non-amortisation of intangible assets which have an indefinite useful life.

Those standards that have reduced the national GAAP profit have also done so for a variety of reasons. For example, *IAS 12* requires the use of the 'temporary difference' approach when calculating any deferred tax liability; this is different from the 'timing difference' approach that has historically been applied in the UK and Ireland. Although the difference in these approaches is likely to account for a proportion of the decrease in the profit calculated under *IAS 12*, it is also likely that many of the other IFRS adjustments will also have had a deferred tax effect. However, in Italy the approach under national GAAP was similar to IFRS; thus the impact is a consequence of the other IFRS adjustments. This decrease in profit from the figure reported under national GAAP, which is attributable to *IAS 17*, is likely to be due to the re-classification of some leases under the international standard as either finance or operating leases. The *IAS 17* definition of a finance lease is less stringent than that provided by the previous standard in the UK and Ireland (*SSAP 21*) as the international standard does not contain any numerical guidelines. As a result, certain leases that were classified as operating leases under national GAAP may have been re-classified as finance leases under *IAS 17*. In Italy the definition of a finance lease included in the national accounting standards (*OIC 1* and *OIC 17*) was similar to that used in *IAS 17*. However, for some companies, the impact of the new standard could arise from the differences between *IAS 17* and national law which states that the periodic payments of a finance lease should be recognised as expenses on a straight-line basis in the income statement accompanied by an explanation (in the notes) of the impact that the financial method (established by the *IAS 17*) would have had on the income and on the related total assets and liabilities. In general (but not always), the national accounting standards (similar to *IAS 17*) were applied in the consolidated report whereas the national law was applied in the individual company's report. As far as accounting for foreign currency is concerned, *IAS 21* was revised in 2003 to provide additional guidance on the translation method and on the determination of the functional and presentation currencies. The objective of the revision was to reduce or eliminate alternative accounting treatments, redundancies and conflicts. Under UK and Irish GAAP it was possible to recognise some foreign currency gains or losses in the balance sheet reserves, however, under IFRS, the majority of these gains and losses now have to be recognised in the income statement. In Italy a similar change has occurred after the reform of company law by decree no. 6/2003.

Table 4.3 Descriptive statistics of the IFRS equity adjustments

	Mean	SD	Median	Min	Max	Skew	Kurt
Total Equity per national GAAP	100.00	0.00	100.00	100.00	100.00	N/A	N/A
IFRS 2	0.15	0.39	0.00	-0.41	1.89	2.97	9.46
IFRS 3	-11.26	140.41	0.29	-1489.40	30.16	-10.60	112.60
IFRS 4	-0.14	1.62	0.00	-14.70	6.70	-6.25	62.78
IFRS 5	0.00	0.00	0.00	0.00	0.00	N/A	N/A
IAS 1	0.16	1.74	0.00	0.00	18.48	10.63	113.00
IAS 10	4.63	19.88	2.32	-56.18	198.57	8.19	83.11
IAS 12	-1.99	13.30	0.00	-90.20	58.12	-1.53	22.08
IAS 16	0.52	2.31	0.00	-3.34	16.93	4.69	26.92
IAS 17	-0.53	2.45	0.00	-20.85	0.89	-6.47	47.06
IAS 18	-0.21	1.45	0.00	-11.65	1.94	-6.94	50.04
IAS 19	-6.20	25.64	-0.70	-199.90	80.00	-3.98	31.89
IAS 21	0.01	0.15	0.00	-0.63	1.20	4.65	45.19
IAS 28	-0.03	1.24	0.00	-9.36	8.85	-0.59	51.65
IAS 31	-0.01	0.20	0.00	-1.91	0.91	-6.77	75.59
IAS 32	-0.13	0.77	0.00	-6.92	1.00	-6.96	56.65
IAS 36	-0.21	1.54	0.00	-15.43	1.26	-9.10	88.49
IAS 38	-2.39	36.20	0.00	-379.88	38.30	-10.29	108.37
IAS 39	0.35	5.55	0.00	-20.83	45.12	4.45	40.72
IAS 40	-0.03	0.19	0.00	-1.91	0.00	-9.41	93.97
IAS 41	0.04	0.45	0.00	-0.07	4.74	10.62	112.91
IAS 32/ IAS 39	0.17	1.82	0.00	-6.31	11.55	3.79	25.37
IAS 27, 28 & 31	-0.10	0.07	0.00	-0.47	0.00	-6.03	35.30
Goodwill	1.36	13.31	0.00	-1.91	141.43	10.60	112.49
Acquired goodwill and intangibles	0.37	2.62	0.00	0.00	26.15	9.00	85.96
IFRS 3 & IAS 38	0.00	0.04	0.00	0.00	0.41	10.63	113.00
Other	1.27	8.75	0.00	-17.16	71.98	5.01	37.61
Opening balance sheet adjustment(s)	-0.09	1.02	0.00	-10.20	3.17	-8.56	88.36
Minority interests	-0.01	0.10	0.00	-1.02	0.08	-10.53	111.59
Total equity per IFRS	**85.61**	**176.22**	**99.85**	**-1710.90**	**503.57**	**-9.51**	**98.96**

Notes: This table reports the IFRS adjustments to the total equity calculated under national GAAP as at 31st December 2004 reported as a percentage of the national GAAP total equity. Specifically, summary statistics are reported: Mean is the average, SD is the standard deviation, Median is the mid-point while Min and Max are the minimum and maximum values. Finally, a measure of skewness (Skew) and kurtosis (Kurt) are also given.

A visual inspection of Table 4.3 confirms some of the interesting findings to emerge from Table 4.2. First, the average total value of equity reported under IFRS is only 85.61% of its value calculated using national GAAP. Thus, the overall impact of implementing IFRS for this sample of companies has been to reduce the size of total equity in the balance sheet by 14.39%. The main adjustments which give rise to this reduction are those associated with *IFRS 3 Business Combinations* (-11.26%), *IAS 19 Employee Benefits* (-6.20%), *IAS 38 Intangible Assets* (-2.39%) and *IAS 12 Income Taxes* (-1.99%). These negative adjustments to total equity are partly offset by the effects of *IAS 10 Events after the Balance Sheet Date* (4.63%), otherwise the adverse impact on total equity would have been much bigger. For some of the sample companies, the information supplied in their reconciliation statements did not permit the allocation of an adjustment amount to one specific standard; in these few cases, the multiple standards are shown in the tables and involve sizeable average percentage values in certain circumstances.

These mean percentage adjustments mask a wide spread of values across the sample companies. The standard deviation figures in some of the rows of Table 4.3 are very large, suggesting that the implementation of IFRS affected various companies in different ways. The four largest standard deviation figures relate to *IFRS 3 Business Combinations* (140.41%), *IAS 38 Intangible Assets* (36.20%), *IAS 19 Employee Benefits* (25.64%) and *IAS 10 Events after the Balance Sheet Date* (19.88%). This impression is confirmed by an analysis of the minimum and maximum percentage adjustment values. The gap between these figures is very big for several of the accounting standards suggesting that the impact of IFRS varied from company to company. For example, the range of adjustments associated with *IFRS 3* goes from a low of -1,489.40% to a high of 30.16% of the total equity figure under national GAAP. The figure of -1,489.40% relates to NSB Retail Systems and is partially explained by a negative equity value under UK GAAP before IFRS adjustments were made; one of the biggest of these adjustments related to *IFRS 3*. For *IAS 10*, the spread of the adjustment ranges from -56.18% to 198.57%.

Perhaps not surprisingly, 12 of the international accounting standards had no material impact on the reconciliation from national GAAP to IFRS for the balance sheet figures. These 12 standards were predominantly, though not exclusively, orientated towards disclosure: *IFRS 5 Non-current Assets Held for Sale and Discontinued Operations*; *IAS 7 Cash Flow Statements*; *IAS 8 Accounting Policies, Changes in Accounting Estimates and Errors*; *IAS 11 Construction Contracts*; *IAS 14 Segment Reporting*; *IAS 20 Accounting for Government Grants*; *IAS 24 Related Party Transactions*; *IAS 26 Accounting and Reporting by Retirement Benefit Plans*; *IAS 29 Financial Reporting in Hyperinflationary Economies*; *IAS 30 Disclosures in the Financial Statements of Banks and Similar Financial Institutions*; *IAS 33 Earnings per Share*; and *IAS 34 Interim Financial Reporting*. In addition to these 12, only relatively small percentage adjustments were attributable to *IFRS 1*, *IAS 2*, *IAS 11*, *IAS 23*, *IAS 27* and *IAS 37*. The data for these standards are not shown separately in Table 4.3 but combined into the 'Other' category. Further, the data for *IAS 32* is also included with that for *IAS 39* as it was sometimes difficult to attribute adjustments to one standard rather than the other. Finally, although no adjustment for total equity was documented for *IFRS 5*, it was included in the table to maintain comparability with Table 4.2.

All of the skewness and kurtosis statistics are statistically significant at the 5% level suggesting that the percentage adjustments are not normally distributed across the sample of companies. Some 16 were positively skewed indicating a tail of large positive adjustments while 26 were negatively skewed implying a tail of sizeable negative adjustments; skewness could not be calculated for 11 of the adjustments since a sufficient number of non-zero values were not present. As a result, care must be exercised when studying the mean adjustment values since the numbers may be influenced by outliers; thus, the median statistics are also provided in Table 4.3. An inspection of these statistics indicates that the impact of IFRS adjustments is only -0.15 per cent for the median company in the sample.

As with the income statement analysis, it has not been possible to provide a single reason as to why some international standards have had such a negative impact on the total equity in the balance sheet. For some standards, the reason for the difference is obvious while, for others, it is not quite so clear. For example, although *IAS 19* applies to a broad spectrum of employee post-retirement benefits, it has had the biggest impact on accounting for defined benefit pension plans (Fox *et al.*, 2007). The standard requires an enterprise to recognise both the plan's assets and its liabilities on the balance sheet and many of the UK pension plans were in deficit before and during 2004. Previously, under UK GAAP, companies were permitted to disclose these numbers in the notes to the accounts only; a reduction in the equity figure calculated under national GAAP upon the application of *IAS 19* is therefore understandable. However, in the same year, a new standard - *FRS 17 Retirement Benefits* - became fully effective in the UK, which also required the recognition of the pension scheme deficits/surpluses on the balance sheet of UK companies not applying IFRS.

In contrast to this simple explanation, Bonham *et al.* (2004) point out that *IFRS 3* clarifies the criteria for recognising intangible assets and ensures that more intangible assets are recognised separately from goodwill. The smaller goodwill asset which results is then subject to impairment reviews as prescribed by *IAS 36*. Therefore, the application of *IFRS 3* should create (i) a goodwill asset that is smaller than that which would have been reported under UK, Italian and Irish GAAP and which cannot be written off unless it is impaired; and (ii) a larger intangible asset that is separate from goodwill. In theory, this should increase both the equity in the balance sheet and the profit in the income statement; however, the results reported here show that, whilst *IFRS 3* has increased profit, it has also decreased equity. This decrease in equity is mainly attributable to two outliers (NSB Retail Systems and Rentokil Initial); without them, the *IFRS 3* adjustment would have been positive (1.86%).

As explained previously, the impact of *IAS 10*, *IAS 12* and *IAS 38* is more likely to be attributable to individual company circumstances and the options available within these accounting standards. In Italy the impact of *IAS 38* is due to the differences between the international accounting standard and Italian GAAP. Interestingly, *IFRS 3*, *IAS 12* and *IAS 19* were also amongst the IFRSs identified by Aisbitt (2006) as having the largest negative impact on equity calculated under UK GAAP, as described in chapter two.

An index of conservatism

In the second part of the analysis, the IFRS disclosures are examined by means of a 'conservatism' index. This index, which was developed by Gray (1980), is useful for assessing whether there are material quantitative differences in profits and equity reported under IFRS as compared to that reported in accordance with national GAAP. The conservatism, or comparability, index has been used in several studies that have examined the differences in reported figures produced under various GAAP. For example, Weetman and Gray (1991) used the index to examine the effect of accounting principles on profits produced under Dutch, Swedish, UK and US GAAP while Weetman and Gray (1990) and Weetman *et al.* (1998) studied the impact of UK and US accounting principles on reported profits. Other studies have examined the figures reported under various European accounting regimes (Emenyonu and Gray, 1992; Cañibano and Mora, 2000).

To examine the extent of the differences in profit reported using national GAAP and IFRS, the index is calculated as:

$$1 - \left(\frac{\text{Profit IFRS} - \text{Profit National GAAP}}{|\text{Profit IFRS}|} \right)$$

Similarly, to assess the extent of the differences in equity reported using national GAAP and IFRS, the index is calculated as:

$$1 - \left(\frac{\text{Equity IFRS} - \text{Equity National GAAP}}{|\text{Equity IFRS}|} \right)$$

If the index assumes a value greater than one, this indicates that profits or equity reported using national GAAP are less 'conservative' than those reported using IFRS. By contrast, an index value of less than one means that national GAAP-based figures are more 'conservative' than those produced using IFRS. An index value equal to one indicates neutrality between national GAAP-based and IFRS-based figures.

In addition to calculating an overall index of conservatism for profit and equity, the relative effect of individual adjustments required under each international accounting standard is also examined by constructing partial indices as:

$$1 - \left(\frac{\text{Partial adjustment}}{|\text{Profit IFRS}|} \right)$$

and

$$1 - \left(\frac{\text{Partial adjustment}}{|\text{Equity IFRS}|} \right)$$

The above equations are used to calculate index values for each of the sample companies, where the partial adjustment refers to the adjustment required under each individual international accounting standard. The index values are then averaged across the companies for each of the three sample countries and the results reported in Table 4.4 for the income statement and in Table 4.6 for the balance sheet. Tables 4.4 and 4.6 show, for each country, the mean and standard deviation for the overall conservatism index as well as for some of the partial indices. Partial index values were calculated for each standard. However, to allow the reader to focus on those standards which gave rise to sizeable adjustments for the sample companies, those standards which had a partial index value of one, or very close to one, are not reported separately in Tables 4.4 and 4.6.

The tables also report the results from a t-test that is used to determine whether the mean index values are significantly different from the neutral value of one. To guard against the possibility that outlying index values may distort the mean results, medians were also calculated and a non-parametric Wilcoxon signed ranks test was conducted. These statistics are not reported in the current monograph because of space considerations but where differences from the mean results emerged, these are commented upon. The Wilcoxon test was used to determine whether the median index values were significantly different from the neutral value of one.

Perhaps the most salient point arising from an examination of Table 4.4 relates to the mean index values that were calculated for the profit figures reported under IFRS and national GAAP. In particular, the table shows that, on average, the profit reported under IFRS for the sample companies was higher than that reported using either UK, Italian or Irish GAAP. More specifically, the results show that profits under UK, Italian and Irish GAAP were only 66.1%, 84.6% and 89.1% of their value under IFRS, respectively. Furthermore, reported profits under UK and Italian GAAP were significantly less than those reported using IFRS at the 1% and 10% level, respectively; the p-value for the UK conservatism index is 0.000, while the corresponding figure for the Italian conservatism index is 0.097. Thus, the results suggest that IFRS had a significant impact on the reported profits of UK and Italian companies, although the impact was greater for the UK companies in the sample.

Table 4.4 Index of conservatism - income statement

Index	UK		
	Mean	SD	p-value
Profit	0.661	0.719	0.000***
IFRS 2	0.999	0.203	0.995
IFRS 3	0.792	0.548	0.001***
IFRS 4	0.999	0.004	0.305
IFRS 5	0.998	0.013	0.198
IAS 1	0.992	0.069	0.259
IAS 10	0.947	0.322	0.125
IAS 12	1.015	0.101	0.170
IAS 16	1.007	0.048	0.146
IAS 17	0.991	0.285	0.754
IAS 18	0.992	0.075	0.305
IAS 19	0.997	0.098	0.784
IAS 21	1.038	0.312	0.255
IAS 28	0.999	0.001	0.899
IAS 31	0.997	0.047	0.545
IAS 32	1.000	0.003	0.247
IAS 36	0.999	0.016	0.837
IAS 38	0.966	0.256	0.210
IAS 39	1.007	0.044	0.144
IAS 40	0.955	0.185	0.027**
IAS 41	0.995	0.051	0.325
IAS 32/ IAS 39	0.998	0.064	0.762
IAS 27, 28 & 31	1.000	0.000	-
Goodwill	0.983	0.074	0.031**
IFRS 3 & *IAS 38*	0.991	0.050	0.090*
Unclassified (other)	0.999	0.030	0.705
Minority interests	1.002	0.013	0.148
Reallocations	0.996	0.041	0.320

* indicates significance at the 10% level

** denotes significance at the 5% level

*** indicates significance at the 1% level

Table 4.4 Index of conservatism - income statement (cont.)

Index	Italy		
	Mean	SD	p-value
Profit	0.846	0.460	0.097*
IFRS 2	1.005	0.015	0.080*
IFRS 3	0.815	0.454	0.043**
IFRS 4	0.975	0.092	0.166
IFRS 5	1.000	0.000	-
IAS 1	1.000	0.000	-
IAS 10	1.000	0.000	-
IAS 12	1.007	0.030	0.236
IAS 16	1.005	0.021	0.258
IAS 17	1.002	0.010	0.280
IAS 18	1.002	0.016	0.540
IAS 19	1.035	0.099	0.080
IAS 21	0.999	0.001	0.333
IAS 28	0.991	0.052	0.377
IAS 31	1.000	0.000	-
IAS 32	1.000	0.000	-
IAS 36	1.002	0.015	0.491
IAS 38	0.983	0.095	0.359
IAS 39	1.039	0.136	0.146
IAS 40	1.000	0.000	0.327
IAS 41	1.000	0.000	-
IAS 32/ IAS 39	1.000	0.000	-
IAS 27, 28 & 31	0.980	0.092	0.276
Goodwill	1.000	0.000	-
IFRS 3 & IAS 38	1.000	0.000	-
Unclassified (other)	0.995	0.154	0.853
Minority interests	1.000	0.000	-
Reallocations	1.000	0.000	-

* indicates significance at the 10% level

** denotes significance at the 5% level

*** indicates significance at the 1% level

Table 4.4 Index of conservatism - income statement (cont.)

Index	Ireland		
	Mean	SD	p-value
Profit	0.891	0.220	0.238
IFRS 2	1.010	0.014	0.095*
IFRS 3	0.899	0.175	0.178
IFRS 4	1.000	0.000	-
IFRS 5	1.000	0.000	-
IAS 1	1.000	0.000	-
IAS 10	1.000	0.000	-
IAS 12	0.980	0.053	0.340
IAS 16	1.000	0.000	-
IAS 17	1.001	0.003	0.356
IAS 18	1.007	0.019	0.356
IAS 19	0.993	0.021	0.412
IAS 21	1.008	0.020	0.349
IAS 28	1.000	0.001	0.681
IAS 31	0.999	0.002	0.356
IAS 32	1.000	0.001	0.356
IAS 36	1.000	0.000	-
IAS 38	0.999	0.003	0.901
IAS 39	1.001	0.003	0.356
IAS 40	1.000	0.000	-
IAS 41	1.000	0.000	-
IAS 32/ IAS 39	1.002	0.004	0.356
IAS 27, 28 & 31	1.000	0.000	-
Goodwill	0.996	0.006	0.173
IFRS 3 & *IAS 38*	1.000	0.000	-
Unclassified (other)	1.002	0.003	0.224
Minority interests	1.000	0.000	-
Reallocations	1.000	0.000	-

* indicates significance at the 10% level

** denotes significance at the 5% level

*** indicates significance at the 1% level

Notes: For each of the three sample countries, the table details the mean conservatism index value (Mean), its standard deviation (SD) and the results from a t-test (p-value) that was used to test whether the mean index value was significantly different from the neutral value of one.

The effect of individual international accounting standards also varied across the sample countries. For example, the number of standards that resulted in a statistically significant adjustment was highest (lowest) for the UK (Irish) companies in the sample; significant p-values were obtained for four UK and two Italian partial indices while only one adjustment was significant for the Irish companies. In particular, *IFRS 3, IAS 40* and other adjustments associated with Goodwill, resulted in significant adjustments in reported profits for UK companies. For those UK companies where adjustments were attributed to multiple standards, Table 4.4 shows that the combined effects of *IFRS 3* and *IAS 38* had a material impact on reported profits; these standards resulted in an average increase in profits of 0.9%, which was significant at the 10% level. *IFRS 2* and *IFRS 3* had a material impact on the reported profits of Italian companies. For the Irish companies in the sample, significant adjustments in profits were required under *IFRS 2*.

Further examination of these results reveals that some of the standards had a similar impact on the income statement of companies from different countries. For example, *IFRS 2 Share-based Payment* had a significant impact on the income statement of Italian and Irish companies while *IFRS 3 Business Combinations* had a significant impact on the income statement of UK and Italian companies. This difference between the UK and Ireland might have been because of the small sample size. In addition, the impact of these standards on reported profits was similar across countries. That is, *IFRS 2* had a negative effect on the profits reported by Italian and Irish companies; profits under national GAAP were 1.0% (Irish companies) and 0.5% (Italian companies) higher than under IFRS because of the differences in the treatment of share-based payments. By contrast, *IFRS 3*, which deals with business combinations, increased the profits of UK and Italian companies, with the profit under national GAAP being 79.2% and 81.5% of the profit under IFRS, respectively.

An analysis of the results also indicates that several standards had no effect on the profits reported by UK, Italian and Irish companies. In particular, the findings show that UK companies were unaffected by 11 international standards, while 17 international standards had no impact on the reported profits of Italian companies and 21 international standards required no adjustment to the profit figures reported under Irish GAAP[1]. Eleven of these 'zero impact' standards were common to companies in all three countries (*IAS 7*, *IAS 8*, *IAS 11*, *IAS 14*, *IAS 20*, *IAS 24*, *IAS 26*, *IAS 29*, *IAS 30*, *IAS 33* and *IAS 34*).

The median index values and the results from the Wilcoxon signed ranks test largely confirm the findings from Table 4.4 that: (i) profits reported under IFRS were higher than those reported using national GAAP; and (ii) *IFRS 2* and *IFRS 3* had a material impact on the reported profits of the sample companies. However, an examination of the median index values also suggests that reported profits were significantly affected by *IAS 10*, *IAS 39*, *IAS 40* and Goodwill in the UK and *IAS 37*, *IAS 38* and *IAS 39* in Italy, but no further standards were seen to have a significant impact on the profits reported by Irish companies.

Given that the outlying values may be of greater interest to corporate stakeholders than those values which are more representative of the whole (Weetman and Gray, 1990; 1991), the index values were classified into different levels of materiality. Table 4.5 shows, for each country, the number of companies which recorded an index value in each level of accounting materiality, where the 5% and 10% levels of profit were adopted as materiality limits. The table illustrates clearly the dramatic effect that a change in accounting policy can have on reported profits. For example, the distribution of values for the overall conservatism index is skewed heavily towards a less conservative IFRS reported profit. As the table highlights, 51 of the 88 UK companies and 11 of the 27 Italian companies included in the analysis reported a sizeable increase in profits, of 10% or more, under the new IFRS regime. Nevertheless, the table also shows that a small number of companies recorded significantly lower profits under IFRS as compared to national GAAP; seven UK and two Italian companies had profits which were at least 10% lower under IFRS or higher. This finding corroborates the results reported earlier which indicates that the implementation of IFRS affected various companies in different ways.

Table 4.5 Levels of materiality - income statement

	National figure 10% or more below IFRS figure			National figure 5% or more below IFRS figure but less than 10% below			National figure within +/-5% of IFRS figure			National figure 5% or more above IFRS figure but less than 10% above			National figure 10% or more above IFRS figure		
	UK	IT	IR	UK	IT	IR	UK	IT	IR	UK	IT	IR	UK	IT	IR
Profit	51	11	2	6	3	-	19	11	3	5	-	2	7	2	-
IFRS 1	-	-	-	-	-	-	88	27	7	-	-	-	-	-	-
IFRS 2	2	-	-	-	-	-	73	26	7	7	1	-	6	-	-
IFRS 3	32	10	2	3	6	1	51	11	4	1	-	-	1	-	-
IFRS 4	-	2	-	-	-	-	88	25	7	-	-	-	-	-	-
IFRS 5	-	-	-	2	-	-	86	27	7	-	-	-	-	-	-
IAS 1	2	-	-	-	-	-	86	27	7	-	-	-	-	-	-
IAS 2	-	-	-	-	-	-	88	27	7	-	-	-	-	-	-
IAS 7	-	-	-	-	-	-	88	27	7	-	-	-	-	-	-
IAS 8	-	-	-	-	-	-	88	27	7	-	-	-	-	-	-
IAS 10	3	-	-	-	-	-	85	27	7	-	-	-	-	-	-
IAS 11	-	-	-	-	-	-	88	27	7	-	-	-	-	-	-
IAS 12	5	-	1	5	-	-	64	24	6	4	3	-	10	-	-
IAS 14	-	-	-	-	-	-	88	27	7	-	-	-	-	-	-
IAS 16	-	-	-	-	-	-	84	25	7	3	2	-	1	-	-
IAS 17	1	-	-	-	-	-	85	27	7	-	-	-	2	-	-
IAS 18	1	-	-	-	-	-	87	26	6	-	1	-	-	-	-
IAS 19	4	-	-	2	1	-	76	22	7	2	-	-	-	4	-
IAS 20	-	-	-	-	-	-	88	27	7	-	-	-	-	-	-
IAS 21	-	-	-	1	-	-	83	27	6	2	-	-	2	-	-
IAS 23	-	-	-	-	-	-	88	27	7	-	-	-	-	-	-
IAS 24	-	-	-	-	-	-	88	27	7	-	-	-	-	-	-
IAS 26	-	-	-	-	-	-	88	27	7	-	-	-	-	-	-
IAS 27	-	-	-	-	1	-	88	26	7	-	-	-	-	-	-
IAS 28	-	1	-	-	-	-	88	26	7	-	-	-	-	-	-
IAS 29	-	-	-	-	-	-	88	27	7	-	-	-	-	-	-
IAS 30	-	-	-	-	-	-	88	27	7	-	-	-	-	-	-
IAS 31	2	-	-	-	-	-	83	27	7	2	-	-	1	-	-
IAS 32	-	-	-	-	-	-	88	27	7	-	-	-	-	-	-
IAS 33	-	-	-	-	-	-	88	27	7	-	-	-	-	-	-

\- indicates those instances where no companies reported materially different figures under IFRS

Table 4.5 Levels of materiality - income statement (cont.)

	National figure 10% or more below IFRS figure			National figure 5% or more below IFRS figure but less than 10% below			National figure within +/- 5% of IFRS figure			National figure 5% or more above IFRS figure but less than 10% above			National figure 10% or more above IFRS figure		
	UK	IT	IR	UK	IT	IR	UK	IT	IR	UK	IT	IR	UK	IT	IR
IAS 34	-	-	-	-	-	-	88	27	7	-	-	-	-	-	-
IAS 36	1	-	-	-	-	-	85	27	7	2	-	-	-	-	-
IAS 37	1	1	-	-	1	-	87	20	7	-	3	-	-	2	-
IAS 38	5	2	-	-	2	-	79	22	7	1	-	-	3	1	-
IAS 39	-	1	-	1	-	-	84	22	7	1	1	-	2	3	-
IAS 40	6	-	-	-	-	-	82	27	7	-	-	-	-	-	-
IAS 41	1	-	-	-	-	-	87	27	7	-	-	-	-	-	-
IAS 28/ IAS 31	-	-	-	-	-	-	88	27	7	-	-	-	-	-	-
IAS 32/ IAS 39	2	-	-	1	-	-	83	27	7	1	-	-	1	-	-
IAS 27, 28 & *31*	-	1	-	-	-	-	88	26	7	-	-	-	-	-	-
Goodwill	7	-	-	3	-	-	76	27	7	1	-	-	1	-	-
Acquired goodwill and intangibles	3	-	-	-	-	-	85	27	7	-	-	-	-	-	-
IFRS 4 & *IAS 39*	-	-	-	-	-	-	88	27	7	-	-	-	-	-	-
IFRS 3 & *IAS 38*	-	-	-	-	-	-	87	27	7	-	-	-	1	-	-
IAS 28 & *IAS 21*	-	-	-	-	-	-	88	27	7	-	-	-	-	-	-
IAS 27, 28 & 31	-	-	-	-	-	-	88	27	7	-	-	-	-	-	-
Unclassified (other)	2	2	-	1	3	-	84	18	7	-	-	-	1	4	-
Minority interests	-	-	-	-	-	-	86	27	7	1	-	-	1	-	-
Reallocations	1	-	-	-	-	-	87	27	7	-	-	-	-	-	-
Asset swaps	-	-	-	-	-	-	88	27	7	-	-	-	-	-	-

- indicates those instances where no companies reported materially different figures under IFRS

Notes: This table provides information on the distribution of index values across the three sample countries for the whole index and each partial index. The table shows the number of companies within each sample and how materially their profits were affected by the transition to IFRS. The index values are grouped according to materiality, based on limits of 5% and 10%.

A similar analysis of the balance sheet net equity adjustments to IFRS was also conducted; some of the results from this exercise are reported in Table 4.6. In particular, the table details the mean index value, its standard deviation and the results from a t-test that was conducted to determine if the mean values were significantly different from the neutral value of one. The results are shown for the equity index and for the partial indices of those standards highlighted in Table 4.3 for each of the three sample countries. One key finding to emerge from an examination of this table is that the impact of IFRS adjustments to national GAAP is not common across all three countries. For example, the effect of IFRS adjustments on Italian companies was to increase total equity; the mean index value was 0.969, indicating that national GAAP-based total equity was 96.9% of its value under IFRS. By contrast, implementation of IFRS had a negative effect on the total equity of UK and Irish companies; on average, total equity under national GAAP was 53.3% higher for UK companies and 6.1% for Irish companies than under IFRS. However, it should be noted that there was considerable variation in the impact of IFRS on the equity of the sample companies; the standard deviation of the index values is sizeable at 423.9% for UK companies, 12.7% for Italian companies and 5.6% for Irish companies.

Table 4.6 Index of conservatism - net equity

Index	UK		
	Mean	SD	p-value
Equity	1.533	4.239	0.231
IFRS 2	0.998	0.008	0.007***
IFRS 3	0.960	0.149	0.012**
IFRS 4	1.000	0.003	0.320
IFRS 5	1.000	0.000	0.320
IAS 1	0.998	0.017	0.320
IAS 10	0.867	0.623	0.042**
IAS 12	1.036	0.505	0.492
IAS 16	0.989	0.077	0.155
IAS 17	1.038	0.316	0.249
IAS 18	1.003	0.020	0.231
IAS 19	1.674	4.607	0.164
IAS 21	0.999	0.004	0.595
IAS 28	1.001	0.011	0.323
IAS 31	1.000	0.002	0.508
IAS 32	1.001	0.008	0.414
IAS 36	1.000	0.003	0.231
IAS 38	0.988	0.041	0.008***
IAS 39	1.015	0.115	0.227
IAS 40	1.000	0.002	0.143
IAS 41	0.999	0.005	0.296
IAS 32/ IAS 39	0.997	0.057	0.615
IAS 27, 28 & 31	1.000	0.000	-
Goodwill	0.995	0.033	0.141
Acquired goodwill and intangibles	0.996	0.025	0.100
IFRS 3 & IAS 38	0.998	0.018	0.385
Unclassified (other)	1.002	0.030	0.544
Opening b/s adjustment(s)	1.001	0.013	0.347
Minority interests	1.000	0.000	0.320

* indicates significance at the 10% level

** denotes significance at the 5% level

*** indicates significance at the 1% level

Table 4.6 Index of conservatism - net equity (cont.)

Index	Italy		
	Mean	SD	p-value
Equity	0.969	0.127	0.219
IFRS 2	0.999	0.001	0.769
IFRS 3	0.974	0.050	0.012**
IFRS 4	1.004	0.027	0.433
IFRS 5	1.000	0.000	-
IAS 1	1.000	0.000	-
IAS 10	1.000	0.000	-
IAS 12	0.989	0.059	0.321
IAS 16	0.987	0.032	0.047**
IAS 17	1.000	0.003	0.608
IAS 18	1.005	0.022	0.221
IAS 19	1.017	0.044	0.057*
IAS 21	1.000	0.000	0.214
IAS 28	0.998	0.016	0.604
IAS 31	1.000	0.000	0.327
IAS 32	1.003	0.007	0.027**
IAS 36	1.006	0.021	0.138
IAS 38	0.990	0.089	0.574
IAS 39	0.988	0.100	0.541
IAS 40	1.000	0.001	0.327
IAS 41	1.000	0.000	-
IAS 32/ IAS 39	1.000	0.000	-
IAS 27, 28 & 31	1.001	0.001	0.084*
Goodwill	1.000	0.000	-
Acquired goodwill and intangibles	1.000	0.000	-
IFRS 3 & IAS 38	1.000	0.000	-
Unclassified (other)	0.997	0.031	0.674
Opening b/s adjustment(s)	1.000	0.000	-
Minority interests	1.000	0.000	-

* indicates significance at the 10% level

** denotes significance at the 5% level

*** indicates significance at the 1% level

Table 4.6 Index of conservatism - net equity (cont.)

Index	Ireland		
	Mean	SD	p-value
Equity	1.061	0.056	0.046**
IFRS 2	0.999	0.001	0.313
IFRS 3	0.976	0.039	0.187
IFRS 4	1.000	0.000	-
IFRS 5	1.000	0.000	-
IAS 1	1.000	0.000	-
IAS 10	0.955	0.043	0.051*
IAS 12	1.066	0.131	0.272
IAS 16	0.997	0.008	0.363
IAS 17	0.998	0.004	0.363
IAS 18	1.021	0.052	0.363
IAS 19	1.043	0.082	0.257
IAS 21	1.000	0.000	-
IAS 28	1.000	0.000	-
IAS 31	0.999	0.000	0.363
IAS 32	1.000	0.000	-
IAS 36	1.000	0.000	-
IAS 38	0.999	0.001	0.363
IAS 39	1.000	0.000	-
IAS 40	1.000	0.000	-
IAS 41	1.000	0.000	-
IAS 32/ IAS 39	1.000	0.000	0.363
IAS 27, 28 & 31	1.000	0.000	-
Goodwill	0.999	0.001	0.363
Acquired goodwill and intangibles	1.000	0.000	-
IFRS 3 & IAS 38	1.000	0.018	-
Unclassified (other)	1.010	0.013	0.120
Opening b/s adjustment(s)	1.000	0.000	-
Minority interests	1.002	0.004	0.363

* indicates significance at the 10% level

** denotes significance at the 5% level

*** indicates significance at the 1% level

Notes: For each of the three sample countries, the tables detail the mean conservatism index value (Mean), its standard deviation (SD) and the results from a t-test that was used to test whether the mean index value was significantly different from the neutral value of one.

In terms of the number of adjustments required, Table 4.6 indicates that the implementation of IFRS had a greater impact on the balance sheets of UK companies than either Italian or Irish companies. In particular, for UK companies, 15 of the standards required adjustments to be made to reported equity, while adjustments in order to comply with IFRS were required for only 12 and 10 standards for Italian and Irish companies, respectively. Although Table 4.6 indicates that several standards had an impact on the balance sheets of the sample companies, only a few resulted in significant adjustments. More specifically, only five of the standards had a significant impact on the reported equity of Italian companies, compared to four standards for UK companies and only one standard resulted in a significant adjustment for Irish companies. Closer examination of these standards reveals that their impact differed across the sample countries. In particular, while *IFRS 2 Share-based Payment* and *IAS 38 Intangible Assets* significantly increased the reported equity of UK companies, they had only a minimal positive effect on the balance sheets of Italian and Irish companies. Similarly, it was only Italian companies that recorded significantly lower equity as a result of *IAS 19*, *IAS 32* and the combined effects of *IAS 27*, *IAS 28* and *IAS 31*, and significantly higher equity as a result of *IAS 16*. However, the impact of some standards was common across two countries, with *IFRS 3* significantly increasing reported equity in the UK and Italy and *IAS 10* in the UK and Ireland.

The results from an analysis of median index values, which are available from the authors upon request, support these findings. In addition to the significant standards identified in Table 4.6, the results from the analysis of median index values indicate that *IAS 12*, *IAS 17* and *IAS 19* had a material effect on the reported equity of UK companies, while *IAS 37* and *IAS 38* resulted in a significant adjustment to the reported equity of Italian companies.

Table 4.7 Levels of materiality - net equity

	National figure 10% or more below IFRS figure			National figure 5% or more below IFRS figure but less than 10% below			National figure within +/- 5% of IFRS figure			National figure 5% or more above IFRS figure but less than 10% above			National figure 10% or more above IFRS figure		
	UK	IT	IR	UK	IT	IR	UK	IT	IR	UK	IT	IR	UK	IT	IR
Equity	12	7	-	14	3	-	36	10	2	8	3	3	22	4	1
IFRS 1	2	-	-	-	-	-	90	27	6	-	-	-	-	-	-
IFRS 2	-	-	-	1	-	-	91	27	6	-	-	-	-	-	-
IFRS 3	7	2	1	5	1	-	77	24	5	2	-	-	1	-	-
IFRS 4	-	-	-	-	1	-	92	25	6	-	-	-	-	1	-
IFRS 5	-	-	-	-	-	-	92	27	6	-	-	-	-	-	-
IAS 1	1	-	-	-	-	-	91	27	6	-	-	-	-	-	-
IAS 2	-	-	-	1	-	-	91	27	6	-	-	-	-	-	-
IAS 7	-	-	-	-	-	-	92	27	6	-	-	-	-	-	-
IAS 8	-	-	-	-	-	-	92	27	6	-	-	-	-	-	-
IAS 10	15	-	1	15	-	1	62	27	4	-	-	-	-	-	-
IAS 11	-	-	-	-	-	-	92	27	6	-	-	-	-	-	-
IAS 12	4	1	-	3	-	-	61	26	4	10	-	1	14	-	1
IAS 14	-	-	-	-	-	-	92	27	6	-	-	-	-	-	-
IAS 16	2	1	-	1	2	-	89	24	6	-	-	-	-	-	-
IAS 17	-	-	-	-	-	-	79	27	6	10	-	-	3	-	-
IAS 18	-	-	-	-	-	-	91	26	5	-	-	-	1	1	1
IAS 19	1	-	-	-	-	1	56	25	2	12	1	2	23	1	1
IAS 20	-	-	-	-	-	-	92	27	6	-	-	-	-	-	-
IAS 21	-	-	-	-	-	-	92	27	6	-	-	-	-	-	-
IAS 23	1	-	-	-	-	-	91	27	6	-	-	-	-	-	-
IAS 24	-	-	-	-	-	-	92	27	6	-	-	-	-	-	-
IAS 26	-	-	-	-	-	-	92	27	6	-	-	-	-	-	-
IAS 27	-	-	-	-	-	-	92	26	6	-	1	-	-	-	-
IAS 28	-	-	-	-	1	-	91	26	6	-	-	-	1	-	-
IAS 29	-	-	-	-	-	-	92	27	6	-	-	-	-	-	-
IAS 30	-	-	-	-	-	-	92	27	6	-	-	-	-	-	-
IAS 31	-	-	-	-	-	-	92	27	6	-	-	-	-	-	-
IAS 32	-	-	-	-	-	-	91	27	6	1	-	-	-	-	-
IAS 33	-	-	-	-	-	-	92	27	6	-	-	-	-	-	-
IAS 34	-	-	-	-	-	-	92	27	6	-	-	-	-	-	-
IAS 36	-	-	-	-	-	-	92	25	6	-	2	-	-	-	-
IAS 37	1	1	-	-	-	-	91	25	6	-	1	-	-	-	-
IAS 38	4	1	-	1	-	-	87	24	6	-	-	-	-	2	-

- indicates those instances where no companies reported materially different figures under IFRS.

Table 4.7 Levels of materiality - net equity (cont.)

	National figure 10% or more below IFRS figure			National figure 5% or more below IFRS figure but less than 10% below			National figure within +/- 5% of IFRS figure			National figure 5% or more above IFRS figure but less than 10% above			National figure 10% or more above IFRS figure		
	UK	IT	IR	UK	IT	IR	UK	IT	IR	UK	IT	IR	UK	IT	IR
IAS 39	-	3	-	-	2	-	90	20	6	-	-	-	2	2	-
IAS 40	-	-	-	-	-	-	92	27	6	-	-	-	-	-	-
IAS 41	-	-	-	-	-	-	92	27	6	-	-	-	-	-	-
IAS 28/IAS 31	-	-	-	-	-	-	92	27	6	-	-	-	-	-	-
IAS 32/IAS 39	2	-	-	1	-	-	88	27	6	-	-	-	1	-	-
Goodwill	2	-	-	-	-	-	89	27	6	1	-	-	-	-	-
Acquired goodwill and intangibles	2	-	-	-	-	-	90	27	6	-	-	-	-	-	-
IFRS 4 & IAS 39	1	-	-	-	-	-	91	27	6	-	-	-	-	-	-
IFRS 3 & IAS 38	1	-	-	-	-	-	91	27	6	-	-	-	-	-	-
IAS 28 & IAS 21	-	-	-	-	-	-	92	27	6	-	-	-	-	-	-
IAS 32 & IAS 39	-	1	-	-	-	-	92	22	6	-	3	-	-	1	-
IAS 27, 28 & 31	-	-	-	-	-	-	92	27	6	-	-	-	-	-	-
IAS 32, 39 & IFRS 4	-	-	-	-	-	-	92	26	6	-	-	-	-	1	-
Unclassified (other)	-	-	-	3	2	-	88	24	6	-	1	-	1	-	-
Prior year/ Op.b/s adjustment	-	-	-	-	-	-	92	27	6	-	-	-	-	-	-
Opening b/s adjustment(s)	-	-	-	-	-	-	91	27	6	-	-	-	1	-	-
Fixed assets	-	-	-	-	-	-	92	27	6	-	-	-	-	-	-
Hindsight adj	-	-	-	-	-	-	92	27	6	-	-	-	-	-	-
Asset swaps	-	-	-	-	-	-	92	27	6	-	-	-	-	-	-
Minority interests	-	-	-	-	-	-	92	27	6	-	-	-	-	-	-

- indicates those instances where no companies reported materially different figures under IFRS.

Notes: The table shows the number of companies within each sample and how materially their equity was affected by the transition to IFRS. The index values are grouped according to materiality, based on limits of 5% and 10%.

Table 4.7 provides information on the distribution of index values across the sample countries for the equity index as well as for each of the partial indices. Similar to Table 4.5, the index values are grouped according to materiality, based on limits of 5% and 10%. An examination of the distribution of values for the equity index highlights the significant impact that the move to IFRS has had on companies. In total, 41% (11 out of 27) of Italian companies, 37% (34 out of 92) of UK companies and 17% (1 out of 6) of Irish companies had national GAAP-based equity figures that were 10% or more above or below the IFRS-based equity figure. However, the table also shows that the impact of IFRS was very different across companies within a single country. For example, while 24% of the UK companies (22 out of 92) in the sample recorded a national GAAP-based figure that was 10% or more above the corresponding IFRS-based figure, 15% recorded figures based on national GAAP that were between 5% to 10% below the IFRS-based figure, and a further 13% experienced a difference in reported equity of 10% or more below the IFRS-based equity figure. A similar picture emerges from an examination of the distribution of index values for *IAS 12*. While four UK companies reported a material increase in equity, 14 UK companies recorded a significant decrease in equity (based on the 10% materiality limit). These figures highlight that the impact of IFRS on balance sheets varied significantly across countries and companies.

That different international standards have a significant impact on the reported equity of companies from different countries is also apparent from Table 4.7. For example, Table 4.7 highlights that UK companies experienced material differences in equity due to *IFRS 3 Business Combinations*, *IAS 10 Events after the Balance Sheet Date*, *IAS 12 Income Taxes* and *IAS 19 Employee Benefits*. However, the difference in the equity figures of Italian companies was largely attributable to *IFRS 3*, *IAS 16*, *IAS 38* and *IAS 39*. Taken together, Tables 4.4 to 4.7 suggest that any analysis of the impact of IFRS needs to take account of the national jurisdiction of the company. Such a finding is not surprising since the impact of IFRS will vary according to the differences between the national and international accounting standards being studied.

Summary

This chapter has analysed the extent and nature of IFRS adjustments using the Reconciliation Statements that companies were required to produce under *IFRS 1 First-time Adoption of International Financial Reporting Standards*. It did so in two ways: first, by expressing the IFRS adjustment required by each standard as a percentage of the total profit (loss) and total equity according to national GAAP for all countries together, and second, by calculating an index of conservatism for each country. The impact of IFRS implementation on profit was significant; on average, profit calculated under national GAAP increased by a sizeable percentage (48.51%) once figures were translated to IFRS. The main standards responsible for this percentage increase included *IAS 40 Investment Property* and other adjustments associated with goodwill (in the UK only) and *IFRS 3 Business Combinations* (in the UK and Italy). This is countered by the negative impact of *IFRS 2 Share-based Payment* (in Ireland and Italy). These findings, based on percentage changes, were confirmed by the results obtained using an index of conservatism.

The results also show that the introduction of IFRS reduced the equity calculated under national GAAP by 14.39%, although this effect was not common across all three countries; Italian companies experienced a slight increase in equity while the UK and Irish companies in the sample recorded a decrease. The standards that appear to have had the largest effect on the balance sheet were *IFRS 2 Share-based Payment* and *IAS 38 Intangible Assets* (in the UK), *IFRS 3 Business Combinations* (in the UK and Italy) and *IAS 10 Events after the Balance Sheet Date* (in the UK and Ireland). The same is true in Italy of *IAS 16 Property, Plant and Equipment*, *IAS 32 Financial Instruments: Presentation*, *IAS 19 Employee Benefits* and the combined effects of *IAS 27 Consolidated and Separate Financial Statements*, *IAS 28 Investments in Associates* and *IAS 31 Interests in Joint Ventures*. The implementation of IFRS also affected the equity of different companies in different ways and the results show that these adjustments are not normally distributed. Perhaps not surprisingly, some standards have no material impact on equity calculated under national GAAP. These standards are predominantly, though not exclusively, orientated towards disclosure.

ENDNOTE

1 The international standards that had no effect on the reported profits of UK companies included *IAS 7*, *IAS 8*, *IAS 11*, *IAS 14*, *IAS 20*, *IAS 24*, *IAS 26*, *IAS 29*, *IAS 30*, *IAS 33* and *IAS 34*. For the Italian companies, *IFRS 5*, *IAS 1*, *IAS 7*, *IAS 8*, *IAS 10*, *IAS 11*, *IAS 14*, *IAS 20*, *IAS 24*, *IAS 26*, *IAS 29*, *IAS 30*, *IAS 31*, *IAS 32*, *IAS 33*, *IAS 34* and *IAS 41* required no adjustment to reported profits. Finally, the profits of Irish companies were unaffected by *IFRS 1*, *IFRS 4*, *IFRS 5*, *IAS 1*, *IAS 2*, *IAS 7*, *IAS 8*, *IAS 10*, *IAS 11*, *IAS 14*, *IAS 16*, *IAS 20*, *IAS 24*, *IAS 26*, *IAS 29*, *IAS 30*, *IAS 33*, *IAS 34*, *IAS 36*, *IAS 40* and *IAS 41*.

5 The IFRS Implementation Process

Introduction

As part of the study, a number of interviews were held with key stakeholders in the IFRS implementation process from the UK, Italy and Ireland. This chapter analyses the comments of preparers, auditors, regulators and users drawn from these three countries and examines the interaction between the different stakeholders relating to IFRS implementation. In particular, it considers how they planned for IFRS adoption, the operational changes that companies made to implement all the standards, the IFRS standards that companies found most problematic to put into practice and the consultation process that they went through in order to overcome these problems.

Research method

Table 6.1 summarises the key stakeholders that were interviewed for this project. Panel A shows the UK interviewees, Panel B the Italian and Panel C the Irish interviewees. The study chose these three countries because it was assumed that companies in countries with a similar national accounting environment, such as the UK and Ireland, would report similar reporting changes with the adoption of IFRS, and that companies in a country with a very different reporting environment, legal system and culture, such as Italy, would be affected differently by the adoption of IFRS. For example, the UK and Ireland are Anglo-Saxon countries with accounting standards that focus on shareholders, but Italy has a Roman law legal system and a tradition of creditors being the most important users of financial statements. Thus, it was expected that the implementation of IFRS, with its shareholder focus, would require more of a cultural change in Italy than in the UK or Ireland.

The interviews took place during 2006 as companies were beginning to prepare their first set of IFRS-compliant statements. Two of three researchers interviewed all of the UK and Irish interviewees and one researcher interviewed the Italian stakeholders. The researchers attempted to interview a wide range of stakeholders, although they were restricted to those who agreed to participate in the project. Consequently, although a full range of stakeholders were interviewed in both the UK and Italy, no regulators or users were interviewed in Ireland and there was a predominance of preparers across all three countries.

Table 5.1 A summary of the interviewees

Code	Job Title	Company
Panel A UK based interviewees		
UK1P	Accounts preparer	FTSE 100
UK2P	Accounts preparer	FTSE 100
UK3P	Accounts preparer	FTSE 250
UK4P	Accounts preparer	Multinational Investment Bank
UK5P	Accounts preparer	Multinational Investment Bank
UK6P	Accounts preparer	FTSE 100
UK7P	Accounts preparer	FTSE 250
UK8P	Accounts preparer	FTSE 100
UK9P	Accounts preparer	N/A
UK1R	Regulator	N/A
UK2R	Regulator	N/A
UK3R	Regulator	N/A
UK1U	Accounts user	N/A
UK2U	Accounts user	N/A
UK3U	Accounts user	N/A
UK1A	Auditor	Big 4
UK2A	Auditor	Big 4
UK3A	Auditor	Big 4
UK4A	Auditor	Group A (medium sized)
Panel B Italian based interviewees		
IT1P	Accounts preparer	Italian Stk Exc (MIB30)
IT2P	Accounts preparer	Italian Stk Exc (MIB30)
IT3P	Accounts preparer	Italian Stk Exc (MIB30)
IT4P	Accounts preparer	Italian Stk Exc (MIB30)
IT5A	Auditor	Big 4
IT6U	Accounts user	N/A
IT7U	Accounts user	N/A
IT8R	Regulator	N/A
Panel C Irish based interviewees		
IR1P	Accounts preparer	Irish Stk Exc
IR2P	Accounts preparer	NASDAQ
IR3P	Accounts preparer	Irish Stk Exc
IR4P	Accounts preparer	Irish Stk Exc
IR5A	Auditor	Big 4

Note: N/A means not applicable because the interviewee was either a regulator or user.

A semi-structured questionnaire was used to organise the interviews which were all recorded. The interviews were then fully transcribed and analysed manually. Members of the team were allocated certain questions to analyse and thus a question by question analysis was conducted. A spreadsheet was also used to summarise the findings to the closed questions. This chapter reports the responses to the open-ended questions that related to IFRS implementation for which it was not possible to analyse 'yes' or 'no'/'agree' or 'disagree' type answers. Thus this chapter is different in style from chapter six which summarises 'yes' or 'no'/'agree' or 'disagree' answers. The questions analysed in this chapter are summarised in Table 5.2.

Table 5.2 A summary of the interview questions relating to IFRS implementation

Topic	Subject
1	How did you plan for the implementation of IFRS?
2	What operational changes did you make to accommodate IFRS?
3	Which international standards proved to be the most problematic?
4	Which parties did you consult with to overcome the problems that you experienced with IFRS?

Planning for the implementation: preparers

Generally, most of the sample companies in all three countries had started their IFRS preparation in 2003, two years before the effective implementation date and three years before the first set of statutory accounts under IFRS were required. A common approach appeared to be employed by all the company interviewees in the transition to IFRS. First, a project manager or a working group consisting of up to a dozen people was set up, both hereafter referred to as project leaders, and this person, or group, was then responsible for the IFRS implementation. Sometimes, people were recruited externally to fill these roles, but often, internal finance staff members were re-assigned 'to move the IFRS project forward'. In cases where it involved a single person, this role was their sole responsibility, but where a working group was used, the members of the group often had other corporate duties to perform on a daily basis. In some cases the project leader included a Big 4 auditor and this was more likely in the Italian companies that took part in this study. The project leaders tended to develop a strategy paper outlining details of what needed to be done and suggestions as to how this should happen. These included recommendations on IT, systems, bookkeeping and policies, as evidenced by a UK preparer interviewee (UK4P):

> *There were IT implications, there were pure bookkeeping implications, and then there were policy statements that had to be written.*

In some cases, the project leaders had to budget a cost base for the implementation and secure funding and approval before starting the process. The project leaders then organised for all the IAS, IFRS and IFRIC interpretations to be read in detail, paragraph by paragraph, by either the project leaders or by others specifically identified for the task. These others often consisted of specialist teams such as treasury (*IAS 32* and 39) pensions (*IAS 19*) or tax specialists (*IAS 12*), as identified by a UK preparer (UK2P):

> *If there was a standard that particularly affected one of our divisions then somebody from that division headed up the team.*

Whoever was responsible, IFRS implementation involved a great deal of work as noted by an Irish interviewee preparer (IR3P):

> *It was a huge body of work and basically we looked at the standard, said what are the requirements, does it apply to us? If it does, are there options in it, which we need to decide which to pick, or whatever, or is it just straight forward?*

Not only were some of the standards complicated, but it was sometimes difficult to apply them to certain types of businesses, as a UK preparer (UK1P) clarified:

> *All accounting standards are written for the widget manufacturer in Birmingham who has one pension fund and one subsidiary in the UK and one overseas subsidiary and it doesn't work with companies across one hundred countries.*

Further, a UK preparer interviewee (UK2P) complained:

> *Just ...making the standard fit the specifics of how contracts and projects work took a huge amount of time and effort.*

One preparer interviewee (UK5P), mentioned a previous organisation, a bank, that he had worked for in a developing country and noted that:

> *If you applied the laws strictly you would have to consolidate the government!*

In one company, just one person was involved in the whole process; in another, over 200 people had been co-opted to help in the IFRS transition. A UK preparer interviewee (UK6P) noted that they had had 16 different work streams working on the IFRS implementation:

> *There were quite a lot of contractors, IT people, project people, analysts. We had people with business relationships, to change managers... we had sixteen workstreams.*

Analysis of the specific policies that should be adopted was a major task. Some interviewees commented that policies had been fairly vague, but IFRS required decisions to be made about specifics that needed to be documented, as noted by a UK preparer (UK2P):

> *Thou shalt amortise and thou shalt depreciate, thou shalt capitalise and here's a maximum period. But it didn't say and here's specifically what you can capitalise, whereas we've got that now.*

One problem was that, at the date of implementation, not all of the standards had been finally agreed. A classic example of this was *IAS 39*. As an Irish preparer (IR1P) noted:

> *I suppose the difficulties at the time in terms of IFRS was actually trying to establish what the standards were going to be and how big an impact it was.*

A UK preparer (UK2P) added:

> *And peoples views change. And [Big 4 auditor] views on technical issues have developed during the period and we did have to go back and change some of the positions we took…I imagine the politics internally within their firm [auditors] of getting everyone to agree on a set of global issues is probably huge.*

A further problem was that each company had to decide whether all the companies in the group should report under IFRS or whether to publish only the consolidated accounts in IFRS format. One Irish preparer interviewee (IR1P) worked for one of the few companies that decided that all of its subsidiaries should report under IFRS:

We took the decision to implement IFRS right across the group, for all quoted and unquoted... we wanted people to move to IFRS, and to plan on an IFRS basis and to run the business on an IFRS basis.

The decision to prepare parent and subsidiary accounts under local GAAP was often driven by regulatory or tax considerations. However, an Italian interview (IT1P) also noted:

I believe that application of IAS to the parent company's financial statement is more complex than the consolidated financial statement because some problems are still not completely regulated by IAS.

The next stage in the process was to assess each standard and make a decision as to whether or not it was important to that company. Some companies distributed a questionnaire to all their sites in order to establish exactly what each site was doing in relation to accounting changes and to assess the impact of the new standards on their procedures and systems. For those standards that might have an impact on the group, a document was often produced that highlighted the differences between the national GAAP and IFRS, whether any changes were necessary and, if so, how to implement the changes and what the impact was likely to be on the IFRS financial statements and disclosures. In some cases the audit committee was given a document to discuss at Board level. In many instances new policies had to be agreed and disseminated.

The dissemination stage of the process involved internal meetings or 'conferences' of staff drawn from all the regions, subsidiaries, operations and sites of the groups. Sometimes, these 'conferences' were held in various locations throughout the world, including the US, so that all sites could be included. The purpose of these meetings was to inform accounts preparers in all locations about the new standards and policies and, in particular, identify the sort of information that would now need to be gathered when producing consolidated IFRS reports. The subsidiaries needed to understand how the new reporting standards would affect them.

The next stage of the process was to gather data in order to determine the opening IFRS accounting position and to quantify the changes from national GAAP. Two procedures were employed when determining the opening IFRS position: cut-over; and conversion. Cut-over involved changing the systems and writing new charts of accounts to deal with all the new technical requirements. Conversion was the process of getting the actual numbers changed on the systems. One UK preparer's (UK6P) organisation had a 'conversion' weekend and over £6 trillion worth of adjustments were posted over two days.

One UK company (UK2) had a major problem in determining its opening balance sheet; it had lots of long term contracts and in some cases it had to go back twenty years to work out the opening position:

> *...some of our projects are twenty years long. Trying to work out what decisions would have been made 15 years ago under these rules, so what would have been capitalised, and then rolling it forward to what's on the balance sheet, that was a huge task.*

Overall, an Irish interviewee (IR5A) summarised the implementation by noting that:

> *Everybody got a surprise at the end of it. I don't think anyone was as truly organised as they thought they should be.*

Planning for the implementation: auditors and users

In general, the auditors had started the planning process for the change to IFRS even earlier than their client companies, often pre-2000, as most of them knew that they would be called on by their clients to give advice. Some of the Big 4 were involved in global co-ordination or a European steering group to guide the transition to IFRS. This co-ordination on a global or European basis was essential due to the cultural differences that were apparent in each jurisdiction, as explained by a Big 4 Irish interviewee (IR5A):

> *IFRS is different-culturally different… I think culturally, if that is the right word, a word that means something in UK GAAP parlance could mean something different in French GAAP parlance because we would have learnt it and used it in a certain way. .. Culturally the UK and the British and the Irish mindset is very different to the central European mindset… You can have a lot of pre-conceived notions that you come into it with… we don't have twenty years under our belts anymore.*

This central group then disseminated information to national conversion groups, and Italian Big 4 auditor (IT5A) confirmed that many internal courses were hosted by mainly British auditors because they already had good knowledge of the subject. Specialist groups were also set up to deal with specific, complicated standards such as *IAS 39*, as stated by an Irish Big 4 auditor (IR5A):

> *I think IFRS is a high bar and I don't think the market place was ready for how high the bar was.*

The Big 4 generally held training courses for partners and staff within each national area and geographical jurisdiction in order to update staff and keep them abreast of developments. The Big 4 also developed e-learning packages for staff members to digest. Booklets, manuals, newsletters and technical updates were also prepared to inform staff, and clients, about the transition to IFRS. In addition, partner meetings were held to keep offices abreast of the latest developments.

There was a variation in the level of awareness about IFRS accounting issues among the users interviewed, ranging from large financial companies to an individual investor. The small investor had no idea that there was even a new reporting format. He had noticed that the formats looked a bit different, but was not aware that companies now had to report under a new set of standards. The more sophisticated users, unlike the preparers and audit firms, were unable to give examples of co-operation, either with each other or across their industry; with them it appeared very much to be each user for themselves. For example, many of the analysts were left to update themselves on IFRS if they wanted to learn about it. In other companies, analysts and fund managers were sent on internal and external courses to brief them about the changes to financial reporting. They were particularly interested in how the information that they had previously used was going to be presented in the newly formatted financial statements and if the numbers and ratios would be consistent with those they had previously calculated. In most cases there was a concern that computer models that they had developed might require modification and this was especially so for cross-border investments.

Operational changes: non-bank preparers

Completion of the planning stage resulted in the identification of the operational changes that were required to implement IFRS and these varied enormously from company to company. In one Irish company, no changes had been required at all, but in other companies, IFRS necessitated alterations to many systems and processes. This was especially true in the case of some of the banks, where complete business models and some front office functions, such as trading and sales, had to be changed. Thus, the changes required for banks were very time consuming and very costly, these are considered in the next section.

According to some respondents, the most significant changes by companies in the non-banking sectors were made to general ledger systems, group reporting systems and charts of accounts. The data collection system had to be improved, and the amount of data that needed to be collected increased dramatically. This meant that many of the companies in this study had to completely re-design the forms that subsidiaries and regional offices were required to complete when submitting information for consolidation purposes. This entailed increasing the number of columns and number of lines on these forms and trying to reconcile the new forms going forward to the previous figures from the old forms. As a UK preparer (UK2P) stated:

> *We got into the complexities of the accounts and disclosures. And did we have all the data we needed to do all these 1001 disclosures that were required.*

Some companies installed completely new software applications to capture the data required from around the globe. In most cases, these forms were over 100 pages in length in order to capture all the information needed for the new disclosures. For example, a UK preparer (UK3P) stated that for his company:

> *...all the questions-all the additional disclosure- which is 108 pages.*

In addition, many local entities were still using local GAAP, therefore, organisations had to re-design the collection of data to ensure that local GAAP and IFRS GAAP information was collected.

A number of companies also had to change other systems. The most frequently mentioned of these was the treasury system, and involved the setting up of an automated designation process for hedge accounting under *IAS 39* (UK3P). The share options standard also required models to be employed that had not been necessary before and the use of data information sources such as Bloomberg. However, one FTSE 100 company found that its systems could cope with some of the new requirements; the staff discovered more about its existing systems than they had known before the introduction of IFRS, such as the fact that they could cope with the demands of the new foreign exchange translation requirements (UK2P). Overall, the only other main change required was the creation or amendment of spreadsheets to analyse the vast quantity of information that was being received at head office in advance of consolidated accounts being prepared.

Actual transition to IFRS varied from company to company. Some companies completed their 2004 'close outs' and then changed their systems to cope with IFRS. Management accounts were, therefore, not produced for the first few months of the new financial year until the 2004 sign off when a catch-up phase was implemented to produce the first few months of the new financial year on an IFRS basis. Often the new management information system was based on the existing budgetary system with adjustments required to cope with some of the new major accounting changes. This resulted in the management reporting system during 2005 being a hybrid of the old and the new as managers and the finance departments familiarised themselves with the IFRS figures. The cross-over to IFRS usually commenced with the opening IFRS balance sheet. This balance sheet was then signed off by the auditors so that the companies knew that they at least had an audited starting point for 2005.

The Italian interviewees downplayed the changes to their processes and procedures (excluding the banks), as shown by Italian preparer interviewee (IT1P):

> *It was simply a question of adapting what already existed... the information system...the management accounting systems.*

However, this was because this preparer already had to produce annual reports under US GAAP. Occasionally, the changes required depended on the geographic operations of the businesses. Where operations were in countries that already reported under IFRS, then fewer changes were needed. For example, Poland was mentioned several times as being a country where adjustments were not required as it had been IFRS compliant before 2005. Also, companies with a US listing were sometimes less affected by the changes as IFRS was closer to US GAAP than UK/ Irish or Italian GAAP. Indeed, an Irish interviewee (IR2P) found it easier to report under IFRS than Irish/UK GAAP. The adjustments, in this case, to get from US GAAP to Irish/UK GAAP were then all reversed to get back to IFRS.

Other operational changes included the employment of more staff. This was not only because of IFRS but also, for those with a US listing, the requirement of section 404 of the Sarbanes Oxley Act (SOX). Nevertheless, in some cases finance department staff increased by as much as 25% over 2003 and 2004 in order to cope with the new regulatory demands.

Operational changes: bank preparers

Whilst some of the non-bank preparers were relatively unaffected by the implementation of IFRS, this was not the case for many of the banks. The bank employees interviewed in all three countries had to make a large number of operational changes to implement the new reporting rules. One of the biggest problems was implementing the detail of some of the standards that, in practice, became completely immaterial once implemented. An example of this was the amortisation of 'effective interest' on loans. One UK interviewee (UK6P) claimed that the standards were written for very simple operations or 'widget manufacturing in Birmingham'. However, in practice, businesses and especially banks, were not this simple; banks have many loans in several different legal and operational portfolios. In such cases, whole new systems had to be built to cope with the calculation of effective interest.

Irish interviewee (IR1P) explained that, historically, the bank he worked for had used spreadsheets to analyse loans, categorising them by reference to their expected lives and then used this data to generate the accounting entries. However, since IFRS implementation, each loan is now analysed individually and its life amended to alter the spreading profile of the interest. Thus, instead of making accounting entries for interest based on portfolios of loans, each loan now has to be calculated and treated separately. According to the interviewees, the difference in the accounting entries between the portfolio method and the individual method was completely immaterial and yet a vast expense was required to enable each bank to comply with the rules. In the case of a UK interviewee (UK6P), this involved a re-build of the software. An Irish preparer (IR1P) claimed that the effective interest requirement had meant that it was not just a new system that was needed - it required all its existing systems to be changed. Initially the focus had been on the key parts of the system, but the programming of all the branch systems were impacted eventually, and in the case of Italian interviewee (IT4P), the information system had to be completely redesigned.

A whole new system was also required to process fees and costs. In the case of a UK preparer (UK6P), the new system 'backed out' all of the existing accounting entries and posted them back to the accounting system inclusive of the fees and costs required by IFRS. For Irish interviewee (IR1P), the changes were even more dramatic as the whole business process had to change to accommodate the fact that up-front fees were no longer 'booked' as such but had to 'drip' through the income statement. Thus, front office staff saw their profits drop dramatically. They had been used to seeing the up-front fee as part of that month's profit, but now it was being spread over a number of future accounting periods. Therefore, the traders and front office staff had to be completely re-trained to understand the new system and its ramifications for their salaries and bonuses. This problem especially affected the mortgage departments within the banks and the incentives for staff in the front line of the business.

IAS 39 was the standard that had been expected by the researchers to result in major systems changes due to the hedging and impairment evaluation requirements. This was confirmed by Italian interviewee (IT4P) and again new systems were required to cope with these changes. Previously, these derivative products had been analysed on spreadsheets, but now sophisticated systems were required to deal with the intricate details of the 400-plus page Standard. For example, one Irish interviewee (IR1P) claimed that the securities system had to be replaced in full so that the securities could be re-valued and re-categorised for effective interest purposes. For impairment, all the provisioning models had to be reassessed and rewritten.

Inter-company transactions and hedging by branches also caused problems. Often, branches that took on trades with customers could hedge the exposure with central treasury in an inter-company transaction that was accounted for on an accruals basis. However, under IFRS, new systems were required to match the branch requirements to central treasury's transactions. For example, Irish interviewee (IR1P) bought a new package and then had to tailor it to his bank's specific needs. However, the fact that *IAS 39* had not yet been fully agreed and finalised at the time that these systems were being developed caused problems. Thus, banks were implementing new systems and making changes to their whole business without knowing what the final accounting requirements were going to be. An Italian preparer (IT4P) stated:

> *Undoubtedly IAS 39 was the most problematic… due to the delay by the Board and the EU in permitting a definitive application of this Standard.*

Operational changes: auditors and users

Most auditors felt that the changes that they were obliged to make were not that substantial and the major implication was their need for additional staff. This was both in terms of staff with a knowledge of IFRS, although they were very scarce as there were so few specialists around, and of staff in general to service: (i) the increase in accounting advice demanded by client companies; and (ii) to perform the audits of client financial reports in the new format with the new disclosure requirements. A Group A firm auditor interviewee (UK4A) explained that more audit work was required to verify transitional opening balances and that audit checklists had to been revised, standard by standard, according to the level of difference in reporting requirements between UK GAAP and IFRS.

One implication of the move to IFRS was that firms could now use staff seconded from overseas offices as they were all familiar with the same standards. Thus, the mobility of staff within the auditing profession may increase; this may further enhance the global harmonisation of accounting practices in the longer term. Another change was that partner meetings, staff briefings and technical updates had to cover IFRS as well as local GAAP and there was an increased burden upon technical departments. At the same time, firms were adjusting to new international auditing standards (ISAs) and to client demands for meeting the onerous requirements of SOX, especially section 404.

Conversely, the changes for users were minimal. After an initial training and education about IFRS, users merely adapted their spreadsheets and models to incorporate the new changes. Thus, the impact for users was, in general, not onerous.

Problematic standards

As part of the process of implementing IFRS, the companies decided early on which standards would probably cause them the most problems and then set up resources to deal with these particular standards. Some of these problems, and costs, have been covered earlier in this chapter but other issues were also raised. Table 5.3 summarises the twelve standards that caused problems, in order of most problematic standard first:

Table 5.3 Problematic standards

Standards that caused problems for companies	
IAS 39	Financial Instruments: Recognitions and Measurement
IAS 19	Employee Benefits
IFRS 2	Share-based Payment
IAS 12	Incomes Taxes
IAS 38	Intangible Assets
IFRS 3	Business Combinations
IAS 36	Impairment of Assets
IAS 14/IFRS 8	Segment Reporting/Operating Segments
IFRS 4	Insurance Contracts
IAS 41	Agriculture
IAS 21	The Effects of Changes in Foreign Exchange Rates
IAS 11	Construction Contracts

As predicted, *IAS 39 Financial Instruments: Recognition and Measurement* was the standard widely cited by interviewees as being the most problematic, both for preparers and users. The two principal reasons given for this were:

- the changes that had to be made to internal systems, especially in banks; and
- the resulting large increase in disclosures which made the underlying business position difficult to understand.

A UK preparer (UK2P) summed up her opinion of *IAS 39* as follows:

> *Analysts don't understand IAS 39, certainly our industry analysts don't. I'm sure the banking ones I would like to think would. My personal view is that I don't think it fits a corporate. I know all the big-wigs in the IASB firmly believe it does and you can have intellectual debates until the cows come home about what is the right way of doing it, but I actually thought the old way in the UK GAAP of just using the hedged rate to do the transaction was a better way of doing it for a corporate.*

The second most problematic standard according to the interviewees was *IAS 19 Employee Benefits*. Whilst it had had a variety of impacts on the balance sheets of preparers, the most interesting impact was that on the balance sheet of a UK preparer interviewee (UK8P). Bringing the pension deficit onto balance sheet:

> *...raise[d] questions over the levels of distributable reserves in the company and as a result of that [we did] a scheme of capital reduction effectively to convert our share premium and capital redemption to distributable reserves.*

Ironically, the largest creditor of the company was the pension scheme itself and this resulted in the company having to consult with and gain consent from the Pensions Regulator. However, a similar issue would also have arisen for UK companies applying national GAAP, due to the new requirements of *FRS 17 Retirement Benefits*.

The interviewees quoted *IFRS 2 Share-based Payment* and the deferred tax requirements of *IAS 12 Income Taxes* as jointly being the third and fourth most problematic standards. UK preparer interviewee

(UK3P) claimed that *IFRS 2* was a problem for them because it was an area in which they:

> *...didn't have a lot of expertise then and ... needed share option valuations etc so we needed expertise from outside sources on the share based payments.*

Italian interviewee (IT1P) claimed that:

> *This standard [IFRS 2] is clear in theory but from the operational point of view it gave rise to some international discussions concerning its application.*

Conversely, UK interviewee (UK6P) argued that the main problem with *IFRS 2* was the deferred tax calculation in relation to the share based payment.

IAS 12 Income Taxes also seemed to cause a variety of problems. One Irish company (IR3P) maintained that the requirement to provide for deferred tax on 'every tiny difference', although it 'sounds an awful lot easier' was actually difficult for their systems to cope with because previously they had only provided for differences that would not reverse themselves. UK preparer interviewee (UK7P) suggested that the change of accounting treatment of deferred tax on goodwill had taken a lot of 'getting to grips with'. On the other hand, another UK preparer (UK9P) thought that it was an easier standard to implement than the UK standard because there was no requirement to discount any resulting liability. Big 4 auditor (UK1A) commented that the standard itself was not a problem; the problem was the full provision rational behind it:

> *It's a problem because it's a completely and utterly stupid number because you're never actually going to pay that tax.*

Another auditor (UK4A) spoke of *IAS 12* as:

> *...the classic way you've got to unlearn what you knew in UK GAAP and it is not intuitive. It is a standard I don't like at all.*

Issues surrounding accounting for deferred tax in relation to *IAS 38 Intangible Assets*, and *IFRS 3 Business Combinations*, had been widely debated within his audit firm where it was felt that the underlining problem with the standard was the difficulty in understanding its requirements. *IAS 36 Impairment of Assets* and *IAS 38 Intangible Assets* were also mentioned by a number of interviewees as being very subjective, requiring a lot of judgement that made them difficult to implement. An Irish preparer (IR1P) complained that *IAS 38* had proved 'messy' when it came to the classification of certain assets such as accounting software which is 'sitting on a computer'. A UK preparer (UK3P) reported that his company had had an issue over the capitalisation of research and development expenditure that was not previously required under UK GAAP and was concerned whether there was 'consistency' over the group. Two auditor interviewees, IR5A and IT5A, mentioned difficulties that they had experienced with *IAS 36*; it required assumptions about the determination of whether an asset was impaired and highlighted that some judgement was always required to be taken on the auditor's part.

IFRS 8 Operating Segments (previously *IAS 14 Segment Reporting*) was the next most unpopular standard amongst the interviewees, even though this standard was not yet mandatory. A UK preparer (UK8P) stated:

> *[It] was more a case of the extent to which we were having to disclose newer additional information. And it was really just our determination of what the most appropriate segments would be and whether we started off looking at it from a geographical perspective or from a business perspective.*

Likewise, an Irish preparer (IR1P) commented:

> *Segmental reporting we felt was an absolute pain in the rear end to be honest...if we were to fully comply with it actually we would end up with a kind of bitty segmental note and we always intended to give the full segment P&L and then discuss that in the commentary on the results.*

The Italian auditor interviewee (IT5A) also mentioned *IFRS 8* as an area where he had experienced difficulties with respect to the audit, although he had been positive of the effects of this standard in improving predictive ability. An Italian preparer (IT1P) had found this standard problematic because of the information that was required. Segmental reporting appeared to have had a significant impact on Italian companies with both users and a regulator (IT8R) highlighting that standard for specific attention because this information had not previously been required under Italian GAAP. This is obviously a key issue at present with the revised standard requiring segmental reporting to follow the internal 'management' reporting format.

Other problems that were encountered with standards appeared to be more industry specific; for example, an insurance company (IT2P) experienced problems applying *IFRS 4 Insurance Contracts* and a food producing company had difficulties with *IAS 41 Agriculture* in relation to accounting for biological assets. An interviewee from a UK company that competed mainly with US based organisations had been challenged when conforming to *IAS 21 The Effects of Changes in Foreign Exchange Rates.* A UK preparer (UK7P) complained that *IAS 11 Construction Contracts* had also caused a problem as far as the market values of any embedded options contained in long-term contracts were concerned. This had been resolved by reporting these separately in the income statement.

A UK Big 4 auditor (UK2A) alluded to problems with international standards becoming industry specific. Also, a Big 4 Italian auditor (IR5A) mentioned that the financial services industry was a sector that had been significantly affected by the introduction of IFRS and commented that accounting figures relating to pensions, derivatives and fair values generally were very difficult to audit. On the whole, the auditors found the rules-based standards, such as *IAS 39 Financial Instruments: Recognition and Measurement*, more problematic than others.

A UK regulator (UK3R) seized upon the lack of consistency amongst companies in producing their reconciliation statements to illustrate differences in amounts between reporting under their country specific GAAP to reporting using IFRS; he described the resulting documents as 'a nightmare'. However, he conceded that the relevant standard, *IFRS 1 First-time Adoption of International Financial Reporting Standards*, did not require a uniform presentation and that it had served to highlight material changes without readers' attention being diverted to 'trivia'. Another UK regulator (UK1R) stated that not all of the complaints directed at IFRS had been valid.

Consulting others: preparers

To overcome some of the problems associated with the adoption of IFRS, preparers indicated that they had often consulted outside stakeholder groups. For example, all the companies had discussed their IFRS requirements with their auditors, either by seeking advice and help, or by getting approval from auditors for the treatment of certain items in the accounts. Some companies contacted Big 4 firms that were not their auditors to seek their advice. However, the Big 4 firms were not always advanced enough themselves to be able to give advice. As a UK preparer (UK6P) explained:

> *It's lovely to be told that you are the first person that's thought of this problem, but it actually doesn't get your problem solved in your design and build schedule.*

Another UK preparer (UK1P) also believed this to be true of his company's auditors, describing his company as being 'ahead of the game'.

Some of the interviewees thought that there should be more help from the IASB in informing them of which standards to read first and which standards were most relevant to specific sectors.

Some companies approached IFRIC for guidance or made appeals to the IASB for clarification about the treatment of certain transactions or to lobby for changes to the current standards, notably the banking industry with regard to *IAS 39*. The IASB interviewee noted that the IASB had consulted on many fronts including: the European round table; the 100 Group in the UK; the 100 Group in Australia; groups of analysts; the International Organization of Securities Commissions (IOSCO); accountancy firms plus users and preparers, through various working parties. The UK standard setter focussed on more local constituencies, such as the Confederation of British Industry (CBI) and the Association of British Insurers (ABI). Indeed, at some of the IASB gatherings, 'side meetings' developed to discuss issues that remained of great concern to preparers although the IASB had effectively concluded consultation. For example, some of the interviewees who worked with the banks felt that they were getting the message that they had to 'solve [their] own problems'. As a UK preparer (UK6P) noted:

> *There was this little group of very frustrated people having raised an issue 'with the IASB staff' but not getting any answers.*

However, an Irish preparer's (IR4P) communication with regulators had consisted of only one public IASB meeting that had been held in Dublin. This could be compared to some Italian companies where there had been little consultation with the wider stakeholder groups other than auditors, although two Italian preparer interviewees (IT3P and IT4P) had been in communication with CONSOB (Italian Security

Exchange Commission) while none had spoken with the OIC (Italian Standard Setter).

In some instances, sector work-groups or round tables were organised or a relevant trade body contacted to examine the standards that particularly affected a specific industrial sector, as noted by an Italian preparer (IT1P):

> *In our sector a round table was organised with some European companies to discuss the main problems connected with the IAS.*

A UK interviewee (UK2P) had been especially pleased about the industry meetings in his sector as it facilitated a brain-storming of big issues, identified different approaches and gave his company confidence that:

> *...we weren't on our own, out of the issues we had identified, everybody else was identifying, they were taking similar approaches....we weren't going off on a complete tangent from everyone else.*

Trade bodies were also involved in the process, especially in sectors such as banking with The International Securities Dealers Association (ISDA), the British Bankers Association (BBA), Irish Financial Services Regulatory Authority (IFRSA), the Revenue and the London Bankers Association (LBA) all being consulted. Often, these consultations were on particular technical queries such as whether credit derivatives were derivative instruments or guarantees (UK4P). The same happened in Italy: the Bank of Italy and the Italian Association of Banks (ABI) were involved in the transition phase of the banking sector. The FSA was also involved as, although IFRS is an accounting, and not a regulatory issue, the accounting changes affected the regulatory capital reserves requirements for banks. Similarly, some utility companies experienced regulatory problems as ratios of reserves to cash are monitored in the UK (UK5P). In one Italian case, the credit rating agencies were contacted about the approach to various transactions and, in some jurisdictions, central banks were also involved (UK5P). In addition, trade unions were consulted, especially in matters such as pensions and stock options.

None of the Italian companies, apart from one, sought advice from investors, analysts or investment organisations, although investor relations departments within the organisation were occasionally consulted for their views. This was also the case with the investor relations department of IR1P which had been involved with investors and analysts who had wanted interpretations of what the IFRS impact on the accounting numbers was going to be. Investor relations also dealt with analysts who wrote to the bank asking whether the bank agreed or disagreed with their subsequently analysed numbers. These analysts wanted guidance from the bank as to whether the results would be in line with their predictions in order to 'calm nerves.'

Overall, there appeared to be disappointment that stakeholders, other than auditors, regulators and trade associations, had little interest in the change to IFRS. An Irish preparer (IR3P) noted 'really it wasn't exercising people's minds at all'. However, the above evidence substantiates earlier comments that conversion to IFRS has been costly to companies in terms of staff time.

Consulting others: auditors and users

The auditors needed to prepare a great deal for IFRS as they were expected to give advice to their clients and so had to be ahead of the game in many respects. In general, the Big 4 consulted each other through various forums in order to ensure that they all had a similar understanding of the standards; one such forum was the professional Institutes in each country which held meetings to discuss the contents of the standards, how they should be interpreted, and to share ideas. However, as one Big 4 interviewee (UK2A) noted, the Big 4 had to be careful that they were not considered to be a cartel and so they could not really sit down together and arrive at a consensus. The technical offices of the audit firms were very important to the process of change and updated all the regional and local offices about the latest decisions concerning the treatment of items. For example, the Italian audit firm's offices in the study were able to contact the London office for advice on technical matters.

The auditors took an active lead in some of the consultation process by attending or convening meetings for industry groups at a local level and liaising with standard setters. For example, the Big 4 had, on occasions, to contact IFRIC for guidance on certain matters. This system could, however, be abused, as noted by a UK Big 4 auditor (UK1A):

> *Some people like a bit more certainty and as a consequence IFRIC has been asked for rules or guidance or interpretations on some of the most trivial things ever imaginable.*

The major users of financial reports, such as analysts and large investors, often did not really consult about the potential changes that were about to occur. Analysts of non-financial companies were less likely to seek advice than those that operated in the finance industry. For example the analyst at a financial company (IT6U) had a number of meetings with banks as well as partners of the Big 4, seeking clarification mainly of *IAS 39*; however, the other analysts did not consult with anyone. As two different analysts at IT6U noted:

> *In our sector we didn't consult anyone in particular... I can already anticipate that the impact on the equity or the net income, in the non-financial sector, due to IAS, is minimum...* (Non-financial company analyst)

> *I've had meetings with the IRs of a Bank... the meetings were useful...the banks had already devalued their assets at risk of*

> *devaluation before publication of the first IAS interim report... and due to the assessment of investment property at fair value, the overall impact deriving from the IAS was actually positive in the end. In other words, the big negative impact expected by the market didn't occur... IAS 39 has entailed significant effects for the companies both at level of organisation for replacement of the system and at level of performance which is certainly more volatile now than previously.* (Analyst of financial companies)

An Italian user (IT7U) took a more consultative approach involving its trade body, universities, and the Market regulator. Some of the UK users were institutional investors rather than analysts, and they generally either did not consult at all or, at the very most, made enquiries of their investee companies. The National Association of Pension Funds (NAPF) and Association of British Insurers (ABI) also contributed to discussions about IFRS but these bodies were driven more by specific issues. Thus, users consulted in very different ways depending upon their area of expertise and their class of stakeholder group.

Cross country comparison

Perhaps not surprisingly, interviewees in all three countries shared broadly similar experiences during the implementation of IFRS. The main difference in the planning stage appears to be that the Italian preparer interviewees relied more heavily on their auditors than their UK and Irish counterparts. The operational changes required to accommodate IFRS appeared to be less significant in the Italian companies, excluding banks, arguing that, rather than having to re-write whole systems, they merely adapted the systems that already existed. Whilst *IAS 32/39 Financial Instruments*, *IAS 19 Employee Benefits*, *IFRS 2 Share-based Payment* and *IAS 12 Income Taxes* proved to be a problem for both UK and Irish interviewees, the Italian interviewees reported having particular problems with both *IAS 32/IAS 39* and *IFRS 8/IAS 14*. In overcoming these problems the preparers interviewed in all three countries engaged in common approaches to consultation with similar parties.

Summary

This chapter has established that the planning of IFRS adoption varied for each stakeholder group. The majority of companies started to plan in 2003 but auditors started to plan as far back as 2000. In most companies, conversion was driven by a central committee which then disseminated and collated information throughout their group. The operational changes that were made to implement IFRS were greatest in the banking sector although other sectors also experienced changes. The consultation process that stakeholders undertook to attempt to overcome problems was varied and often depended upon their particular sector, such as the banks. Most companies had consulted with their auditors, but practice varied where other stakeholders were consulted or not. The IFRS standards that they found most problematic to put into practice were *IAS 32/39 Financial Instruments*, *IAS 19 Employee Benefits*, *IFRS 2 Share-based Payment*, *IAS 12 Income Taxes*, *IAS 38 Intangible Assets*, *IFRS 3 Business Combinations*, *IAS 36 Impairment of Assets* and *IFRS 8/IAS 14 Operating Segments/Segment Reporting*.

Overall, the process of implementing IFRS had not always been easy. Further aspects of the change to IFRS are examined in the next chapter to explore in more detail whether IFRS has met the IASB's stated objective of providing decision-useful financial reports.

6 The Implications of IFRS Implementation

Introduction

This chapter considers some of the early consequences of the implementation of IFRS that were explored during the interview process described in the preceding chapter and comments on the similarities and differences between the countries and between the different stakeholder groups. The chapter first summarises the consultation process undertaken by interviewees to benchmark and communicate their IFRS disclosures. The next section summarises the importance of financial statement disclosures for a company's reputation. The chapter then considers the costs and benefits of implementation by country and stakeholder group including the impact on the share price, the cost of capital, capital structure and any tax implications, whether the benefits have outweighed the costs, whether companies are worried about giving away strategic information and whether it is now easier to assess managerial performance. The chapter then examines the future impact of IFRS on comparability and harmonisation and concludes with a discussion of decision-usefulness. The results reported in this chapter are based on Table 6.1 Panels A to G which summarise the close-ended interview questions with 'yes', 'no' and 'do not know/ did not answer' by stakeholder category and by country. The information in the table is supplemented by interview quotes to enrich some of these findings.

Table 6.1 Response to interview questions

Panel A

Summary of responses from all preparer interviewees

	Yes	No	Unsure	Total
IFRS consultation during and prior to IFRS implementation				
Wide consultation?	16	1	0	17
With regulators/auditors?	8	1	8	17
With competitors and benchmarking?	13	2	2	17
Much time at AGM?	1	16	0	17
Disclosure				
Does poor disclosure send a bad signal to the market?	8	2	7	17
Good disclosure advantageous to reputation?	8	4	5	17
Capital structure impacted?	1	10	6	17
Costs - Impact on:				
Disclosure of strategic information?	5	11	1	17
Investment, dividend, finance decisions?*	6	10	1	17
Taxation?	4	10	3	17
Share price?	2	12	3	17
Have costs been passed to shareholders?	7	7	3	17
Benefits				
Lower cost of capital?	2	13	2	17
Better assessment of management performance?	6	8	3	17
Improved predictive ability for users?	5	5	7	17
Better company performance analysis by investors?	6	7	4	17
Better informed decisions for users?	8	2	7	17
Overall opinion				
Are new IFRS formats more useful to users?	6	7	4	17
Do the benefits of IFRS outweigh the costs?	0	14	3	17

* Preparers were asked whether IFRS would change company investment decisions

Table 6.1 Response to interview questions (cont.)

Panel B

Summary of responses from all auditor interviewees

	Yes	No	Unsure	Total
IFRS consultation during and prior to IFRS implementation				
Wide consultation?	6	0	0	6
With regulators/auditors?	1	1	4	6
With competitors and benchmarking?	5	0	1	6
Much time at AGM?	0	3	3	6
Disclosure				
Does poor disclosure send a bad signal to the market?	2	2	2	6
Good disclosure advantageous to reputation?	4	0	2	6
Capital structure impacted?	1	2	3	6
Costs - Impact on:				
Disclosure of strategic information?	5	0	1	6
Investment, dividend, finance decisions?*	1	2	3	6
Taxation?	3	2	1	6
Share price?	0	5	1	6
Have costs been passed to shareholders?	4	0	2	6
Benefits				
Lower cost of capital?	1	3	2	6
Better assessment of management performance?	2	0	4	6
Improved predictive ability for users?	2	3	1	6
Better company performance analysis by investors?	1	3	2	6
Better informed decisions for users?	1	1	4	6
Overall opinion				
Are new IFRS formats more useful to users?	2	4	0	6
Do the benefits of IFRS outweigh the costs?	0	4	2	6

* Auditors were asked whether IFRS would affect company investment decisions

Table 6.1 Response to interview questions (cont.)

Panel C

Summary of responses from all regulator interviewees

	Yes	No	Unsure	Total
IFRS consultation during and prior to IFRS implementation				
Wide consultation?	3	0	1	4
With regulators/auditors?	0	0	4	4
With competitors and benchmarking?	3	0	1	4
Much time at AGM?	0	2	2	4
Disclosure				
Does poor disclosure send a bad signal to the market?	2	0	2	4
Good disclosure advantageous to reputation?	4	0	0	4
Capital structure impacted?	0	2	2	4
Costs - Impact on:				
Disclosure of strategic information?	3	1	0	4
Investment, dividend, finance decisions?	0	0	4	4
Taxation?	1	1	2	4
Share price?	0	1	3	4
Have costs been passed to shareholders?	0	0	4	4
Benefits				
Lower cost of capital?	3	0	1	4
Better assessment of management performance?	2	0	2	4
Improved predictive ability for users?	1	0	3	4
Better company performance analysis by investors?	0	0	4	4
Better informed decisions for users?	2	0	2	4
Overall opinion				
Are new IFRS formats more useful to users?	1	0	3	4
Do the benefits of IFRS outweigh the costs?	0	1	3	4

Table 6.1 Response to interview questions (cont.)

Panel D

Summary of responses from all user interviewees

	Yes	No	Unsure	Total
IFRS consultation during and prior to IFRS implementation				
Wide consultation?	3	2	0	5
With regulators/auditors?	2	1	2	5
With competitors and benchmarking?	2	3	0	5
Much time at AGM?	0	2	3	5
Disclosure				
Does poor disclosure send a bad signal to the market?	3	0	2	5
Good disclosure advantageous to reputation?	3	1	1	5
Capital structure impacted?	0	4	1	5
Costs - Impact on:				
Disclosure of strategic information?	2	2	1	5
Investment, dividend, finance decisions? *	0	4	1	5
Taxation?	0	4	1	5
Share price?	0	3	2	5
Have costs been passed to shareholders?	1	2	2	5
Benefits				
Lower cost of capital?	3	0	2	5
Better assessment of management performance?	1	2	2	5
Improved predictive ability for users?	2	1	2	5
Better company performance analysis by investors?	0	0	5	5
Better informed decisions for users?	2	1	2	5
Overall opinion				
Are new IFRS formats more useful to users?	3	2	0	5
Do the benefits of IFRS outweigh the costs?	0	2	3	5

* Users were asked whether IFRS would affect their own investment decisions

Table 6.1 Response to interview questions (cont.)

Panel E

Summary of responses from all UK interviewees

	Yes	No	Unsure	Total
IFRS consultation during and prior to IFRS implementation				
Wide consultation?	17	2	0	19
With regulators/auditors?	3	1	15	19
With competitors and benchmarking?	16	2	1	19
Much time at AGM?	0	13	6	19
Disclosure				
Does poor disclosure send a bad signal to the market?	6	2	11	19
Good disclosure advantageous to reputation?	9	2	8	19
Capital structure impacted?	2	9	8	19
Costs - Impact on:				
Disclosure of strategic information?	13	3	3	19
Investment, dividend, finance decisions? *	2	12	5	19
Taxation?	1	11	7	19
Share price?	2	8	9	19
Have costs been passed to shareholders?	11	0	8	19
Benefits				
Lower cost of capital?	6	7	6	19
Better assessment of management performance?	6	5	8	19
Improved predictive ability for users?	2	5	12	19
Better company performance analysis by investors?	2	6	11	19
Better informed decisions for users?	4	1	14	19
Overall opinion				
Are new IFRS formats more useful to users?	3	11	5	19
Do the benefits of IFRS outweigh the costs?	0	12	7	19

* Preparers and auditors were asked whether IFRS would affect company investment decisions while users were asked whether their own investment decisions would change as a result of the new standards.

Table 6.1 Response to interview questions (cont.)

Panel F

Summary of responses from all Italian interviewees

	Yes	No	Unsure	Total
IFRS consultation during and prior to IFRS implementation				
Wide consultation?	7	0	1	8
With regulators/auditors?	5	1	2	8
With competitors and benchmarking?	3	3	2	8
Much time at AGM?	1	6	1	8
Disclosure				
Does poor disclosure send a bad signal to the market?	8	0	0	8
Good disclosure advantageous to reputation?	8	0	0	8
Capital structure impacted?	0	7	1	8
Costs - Impact on:				
Disclosure of strategic information?	1	7	0	8
Investment, dividend, finance decisions? *	3	2	3	8
Taxation?	4	4	0	8
Share price?	0	8	0	8
Have costs been passed to shareholders?	0	6	2	8
Benefits				
Lower cost of capital?	3	5	0	8
Better assessment of management performance?	3	3	2	8
Improved predictive ability for users?	7	1	0	8
Better company performance analysis by investors?	5	0	3	8
Better informed decisions for users?	7	1	0	8
Overall opinion				
Are new IFRS formats more useful to users?	8	0	0	8
Do the benefits of IFRS outweigh the costs?	0	6	2	8

* Preparers and auditors were asked whether IFRS would affect company investment decisions while users were asked whether their own investment decisions would change as a result of the new standards.

Table 6.1 Response to interview questions (cont.)

Panel G

Summary of responses from all Irish interviewees

	Yes	No	Unsure	Total
IFRS consultation during and prior to IFRS implementation				
Wide consultation?	4	1	0	5
With regulators/auditors?	3	1	1	5
With competitors and benchmarking?	4	0	1	5
Much time at AGM?	0	4	1	5
Disclosure				
Does poor disclosure send a bad signal to the market?	1	2	2	5
Good disclosure advantageous to reputation?	2	3	0	5
Capital structure impacted?	0	2	3	5
Costs - Impact on:				
Disclosure of strategic information?	1	4	0	5
Investment, dividend, finance decisions? *	2	2	1	5
Taxation?	3	2	0	5
Share price?	0	5	0	5
Have costs been passed to shareholders?	1	3	1	5
Benefits				
Lower cost of capital?	0	4	1	5
Better assessment of management performance?	2	2	1	5
Improved predictive ability for users?	1	3	1	5
Better company performance analysis by investors?	0	4	1	5
Better informed decisions for users?	2	2	1	5
Overall opinion				
Are new IFRS formats more useful to users?	1	2	2	5
Do the benefits of IFRS outweigh the costs?	0	3	2	5

* Preparers and auditors were asked whether IFRS would affect company investment decisions while users were asked whether their own investment decisions would change as a result of the new standards.

Consultation process

Consultation and benchmarking

Table 6.1 (Panels A to G) shows that all four stakeholder groups of the interviewees in all three countries considered that they had consulted widely on IFRS. However, users (Panel D) were the least likely stakeholder group to have consulted others. Just under half of the preparers (Panel A) had consulted with auditors or regulators such as professional bodies. It was clear that the interviewees, especially the auditors (Panel B) and the regulators (Panel C), thought that companies had consulted or benchmarked themselves against their competitors, although this was less likely to have occurred in Italy (Panel F). Indeed, as the first sets of IFRS statements appeared, the interviewees commented that it had been useful to review competitor or 'best practice' accounts as part of a benchmarking process. Most of the preparer interviewees looked at the financial statements of other companies, either those who were direct competitors or those companies with a reputation for good disclosure. Alternatively, they used high profile companies, such as Unilever or Glaxo in the UK, although industry peers were sometimes examined for specifics such as their treatment of research and development. This was clearly demonstrated by the UK standard setter interviewee (UK1R) who claimed:

> *One executive of a very large FTSE 100 company said he had spent all of yesterday looking at all of his competitor's financial statements to see what they were doing...*

Indeed, another UK preparer (UK2P) exclaimed that:

> *Everybody seems to have plagiarised everybody elses, which I actually think is really good!*

This preparer continued that there was now a single columnar approach to setting out the statements so that the formats and styles were becoming similar.

UK preparer (UK3P) reflected on how worried his company had been at some organised meetings and presentations when the finance team saw what other companies were doing:

> *...there they were actually presenting what they were doing and I understand they had a whole team basically doing it. It sort of scared us a little!*

However, there was a broad cross-section of views about the usefulness of competitors' accounts guiding financial statement preparation. For example, a UK Big 4 auditor (UK2A) noted that there was too much choice thus hampering any benchmarking:

> *The problem is that IFRS doesn't tell you what you can't do and therefore you can pretty much do anything... the problem is consistency...even within industry it's all over the place... so we no longer [even] have a lot of the strictures and rigours around presentation of the profit and loss account and balance sheet.*

Further, some companies had been put at a disadvantage by being early reporters and one of the first in their peer group to publish their accounts. UK preparer (UK3P) benefited greatly from having a year end other than 31st December and was able, for example, to look at the treatment of intangibles by other companies and see what they were disclosing, what was being capitalised and what was being treated as revenue. His company did not want to be noted for being aggressive in its accounting, or 'get picked up that way'. Another UK preparer (UK2P) also benefited from a different year end and noted:

> *We always had the benefit of being x months behind the bulk of other FTSE100s which was great! Certainly I benefited hugely from being in that position.*

An Irish preparer (IR4P) noted that *IFRS 3* had no benchmark and as the US had a similar standard, she had reviewed US accounts for accounting and presentation purposes.

When benchmarking against other companies, however, a number of problems were noted. For example, the Italian preparer (IT1P) noted that:

> *Hardly any of our European competitors had applied the IAS perfectly.*

And this was echoed by an Irish preparer (IR1P):

> *Now you look at someone's annual report and say- oh- they've treated it that way. I hadn't read that into the standard. Now which of us is right? Which of us is wrong? So I don't think you are going to get real value until maybe five to seven years down the road in the context when things actually have settled down.*

A UK Big 4 auditor (UK1A) also agreed by stating that:

> *We've analysed the FTSE 100 income statements and broadly could barely find two that looked the same.*

However, this view was countered by a Big 4 Italian auditor (IT5A) who stated:

The big groups are often taken as a reference point by the other companies: some of the first IAS-compliant documents published by the biggest Italian companies contained errors and these were repeated in the financial statements of the other smaller companies.

Annual General Meetings

Despite the review of what other companies were doing, there appeared to be very little discussion of IFRS at the Annual General Meetings (AGM). Only one of the preparer interviewees (Panel A) commented that any shareholders had raised a number of questions at the AGM in relation to IFRS. Several interviewees noted that their company had been proactive and had addressed the IFRS conversion process at their AGM presentation, or at a separate forum, and suggested that this might have been the reason for the lack of direct questioning by investors. Amongst the other stakeholder groups, no interviewees were aware of any IFRS issues being raised by shareholders at the AGM. The private investor was unaware of the conversion to IFRS and commented that his decision about whether or not to attend an AGM was not guided by the content of the financial statements but by the selection of cuisine on offer!

Disclosure and corporate reputation

The interviewees were asked whether poor disclosure by companies signalled bad news to the capital markets and other corporate stakeholders and whether good disclosure was advantageous to companies. The Italians (Panel F) wholeheartedly agreed that poor disclosure did send a bad signal, the Irish (Panel G) disagreed while the UK interviewees (Panel E) were more ambivalent. Preparers (Panel A) and auditors (Panel B) were more sceptical about the effect of having good disclosure. However, as preparers and auditors are involved in the preparation of such disclosures, they may not realise the benefits as much as users and regulators.

Some companies tried hard to be open and transparent with investors, as a UK preparer (UK2P) pointed out:

> *[Our company] has a very good reputation within the investor and analyst community for being open and reporting things clearly and that does affect, I guess, how they see management to be performing... there's less likely to be surprises....I can't say it directly relates to a higher share price, but indirectly it must help.*

Another UK preparer (UK1P) explained that the reputation associated with good financial reporting was much more important when brands became associated with a company's name. When a company has many brands that differ from the company's name, there is less risk of reputation damage affecting the business, but when stakeholders associate a brand name with the name of the company, the risk to reputation is much greater.

IFRS did not appear to have had any impact on the capital structure although a UK preparer (UK5P) advised that convertible capital had become unattractive to companies raising finance.

Cost of IFRS implementation

Proprietary information

One possible reason why companies may dislike the imposition of new accounting standards is a worry that proprietary information may be divulged to competitors. The interviewees were asked whether they were worried about the disclosure of strategic information and, while it was clear the UK respondents (Panel E) were worried, the Irish (Panel G) and Italians (Panel F) were far less so. Interestingly, it was the auditors

(Panel B) and regulators (Panel C) rather than preparers (Panel A) who thought that this could be a problem. It may be that the preparers were more knowledgeable about their own operations and could therefore hide strategic information through the consolidation process or could avoid disclosure on the grounds of sensitivity. The IASB regulator (UK3R) thought that proprietary information was of more concern to individual companies rather than groups:

> *You can lose things quite cheerfully in a consolidated account.... like provisioning...you can say we have had legal cases and we made a provision to deal with n of X. If you are a small company and you've just got one case, your opposition says goody that's us, they are providing a million, so let's go for a million. Whereas, it it's a big company, it's just lost.*

An Italian preparer interviewee (IT1P) noted that IFRS disclosures could put a company at a disadvantage in comparison to competitors who did not apply IFRS:

> *IFRS exposes the company more than previously because there is more information, also very confidential information...this favours the market and the analysts but puts the company at a disadvantage vis-à-vis competitors who do not apply the IAS.*

The international standards that possibly compel companies to disclose more information than they previously had done, as noted by interviewees IR4P, UK1P, UK2P, UK2A, IT4P and IT6U were *IAS 36 Impairment of Assets*, particularly in relation to goodwill impairments, *IFRS 5 Non-current Assets Held for Sale and Discontinued Operations* and *IAS 14 Segment Reporting*. For example, Irish preparer (IR4P) explained that when an acquisition is made, the goodwill which may be related to brands is evident. The information that is now provided by IFRS may provide the market with information that could later be used to assess whether the company had overpaid for that particular acquisition. UK preparer (UK2P) noted that:

> *The first time someone has a major goodwill impairment its going to be interesting as to how much disclosure they feel is appropriate. That's where I think that we will be worried, if we ever have one, and ultimately most people will have one at some stage.*

Further, UK preparer (UK1P) noted that discontinued operations could cause a problem if 'you have to do the accounting before you made a public …announcement'. If the company sells, it is telling the shareholders it is a 'duff business', but there is a conflict as the company will want to get the best price, so it is not commercially sensible to disclose this.

A UK Big 4 auditor (UK2A) and a UK regulator (UK1R) commented that segmental reporting for the mid-cap companies had been the biggest concern. They explained that the smaller and mid-cap companies experienced greater problems as many of their competitors were private companies that did not need to disclose any segmental information. The UK regulator interviewed (UK1R) suggested that any standard that required the disclosure of discount rates, expected future growth, expected share price volatility or dividend growth could be a problem. An Italian preparer (IT4P) affirmed that *IAS 14* was a problematic standard due to the information required. However, an Italian user (IT6U) thought that *IAS 14* provided greater disclosure that was not previously presented in Italy and that this information helped to understand the dynamics of net income better.

Investments, dividends, financing, tax and share price

The UK respondents (Panel E) did not consider that any investment, dividend or financing decisions had changed because of IFRS, but there was a more mixed reaction from the Irish (Panel G) and the Italians (Panel F). The users (Panel D) did not believe that any of their decisions had changed, but preparers (Panel A) were more likely to consider that IFRS had impacted these decisions. The Italians (Panel F) and the Irish (Panel G) thought that tax may have been affected by IFRS, but the UK respondents (Panel E) did not think that tax assessments would alter as a result of IFRS. Half of the auditors (Panel B) and one of the regulators (Panel C) thought that there could be tax implications relating to the adoption of IFRS. Apart from two UK preparers (Panel A), none of the interviewees thought that IFRS had impacted on the share price of any company.

IFRS costs borne by shareholders

The Italian interviewees (Panel F) and the majority of the Irish (Panel G) did not believe that any of the costs of IFRS implementation had been passed on to shareholders. Alternatively, several of the UK interviewees (Panel E) acknowledged that these costs were ultimately expensed which in turn reduced the cash flows and distributable reserves available to shareholders. However, some interviewees considered that the extra time and effort that they had personally expended had not been remunerated *per se* by their employers and that they had borne some of the additional costs of IFRS implementation. Indeed, the opinions of both the preparers (Panel A) and the users (Panel D) were split over this issue, whilst the majority of the auditors (Panel B) agreed that the shareholders had ultimately borne the cost. One of the few preparers who believed that the costs had been passed down to shareholders (UK3P) commented that his company had not paid a dividend in the year of conversion, inferring that IFRS conversion costs had contributed towards that situation, whereas the others did not attempt to exemplify the ultimate impact of these costs.

Costs overall

The majority of interviewees acknowledged that IFRS implementation had been costly and all but one of the preparers thought that the IFRS conversion had had a significant cost. Obviously, these costs depended on the size of the company and its domicile but, to illustrate the range, the UK preparer interviewees quoted costs of between £1million and £50million, in Ireland the cost varied from virtually nothing to €100million, whereas in Italy the costs appeared to centre around €1million/€1.4million. In analysing the IFRS conversion costs, some of the preparers conceded that a proportion were likely to be one-off and often non-recurring costs, but also argued that there were additional unquantifiable costs, as exemplified by interviewee IR1P:

> *...some of it will be systems replacement which were eventually going to be replaced at some stage...It cost an awful lot of grief, in terms of a lot of hard work and hours to effect a full consolidation. A lot of work with the audit committee in terms of bringing them through the accounting policies, the changes in accounting policies, being happy that they understood what the differences were and things like that.*

One of the Italian preparers (IT1P), who estimated the IFRS conversion costs to be €1million, was able to attribute these costs to specific standards as follows:

> *..implementation of the models connected with IAS 39, auditing activity on first-time adoption, appraisals connected with application of IAS 16 and the actuarial study for IAS 19.*

Benefits

Cost of capital

One argument for IFRS adoption is that it may reduce the cost of capital. Most interviewees did not think that IFRS would have affected the cost of capital at all, and this was especially true of the Irish (Panel G). The majority of preparers (Panel A) and auditors (Panel B) did not think that the cost of capital had changed, but the regulators (Panel C) and the users (Panel D) did think that the costs of capital would be reduced. A UK preparer (UK5P) commented that if a company's credit rating was altered as a result of revised accounting policies, there would be some impact on its cost of capital. A UK preparer (UK3P) mentioned that credit rating agencies had made adjustments to their grading formulae. This was echoed by another preparer (UK5P) who commented on the credit rating agencies such as Moodys and Standard and Poors:

> *Their rating criteria is dependent on your market discipline and they define market discipline just like how transparent are you, how good is the perception on your financial statements, how good is your corporate governance, so it will affect your rating, it will affect your stock price, it will affect the interest rate that you can get if you want to go and borrow in the market.*

Management performance

A further argument in favour of IFRS is that the provision of more forward-looking information may improve the ability of users to monitor management performance. Indeed, Italian user interviewee (IT6U) commented that this was especially so in the financial sector because: 'The introduction of the fair value allows for better assessment of manager ability.' The views on whether IFRS could help stakeholders assess management performance better were very divided in the three countries, but auditors (Panel B) and regulators (Panel C) tended to agree whilst preparers (Panel A) and users (Panel D) disagreed. As regulators and auditors are more removed from the need to assess management performance, this may have affected the answers that these respondents gave.

Predictive ability, assessing company performance and informed decision-making

The Italians (Panel F) thought that IFRS would provide forward-looking information that could improve the predictive ability of financial statements for users and enable a better analysis of company performance, but the UK (Panel E) and Irish (Panel G) respondents were more likely to disagree and this was especially true of the preparers (Panel A) and the auditors (Panel B). Forty per cent of the users interviewed (Panel D) thought that there was more predictive ability and that it was easier to assess company performance, whilst forty per cent remained undecided; with fewer users being negative, this could be a positive finding in that financial statements are aimed primarily at users. The influence of the Italian respondents (Panel F) is important as the impact of IFRS in Italy was more profound and would have been much more useful in assessing future performance compared with Italian GAAP.

On whether IFRS enabled stakeholders to make better informed decisions, the Italians (Panel F) were very supportive, some UK respondents (Panel E) agreed but the Irish (Panel G) were more negative. This was mainly because of the more negative views of the UK and Irish auditors and preparers. One bank (IR1P) wanted to 'try to educate the market if there is going to be volatility'. There was no particular effort to liaise with other stakeholders as it was considered that there was enough information in the market already; and presentations were often only given to investors in early 2005. The finance departments usually relied on investor relations to give advice on what the market was looking for:

> *So if it was important to an analyst, investor relations guy would be telling us and we would put that into our interim report. [However, not all information was included as] we don't intend to. Why? Because we've a relatively short window for reporting [and] analysts do not pick up our annual report to any great extent.*

Although none of the interviewees had formally communicated with any of the users of their financial reports, five interviewees did not even anticipate any reaction from these users to the newly styled accounts. The response of Irish preparer interviewee (IR1P) obviously reflected the cynicism he felt regarding this issue:

> *Same way as before. When it comes in the post, they put it into the bin – hopefully it's in the re-cycling bin.*

Likewise, another Irish preparer (IR2P) was rather melancholy and offered the following comment:

> *We don't send it anywhere. I have a room up there with boxes... there's a minimum run for getting the glossy done, it's like a thousand or something, they're all piled up, piled up in a room, it's very sad!*

Two Italian preparers felt that it was too early to gauge any reaction from the users of their accounts. While Italian interviewee (IT1P) reported that Italian analysts had been appreciative of the revised reports initially, another Italian preparer (IT3P) felt that the reports were met with scepticism from users who had expected to see the immediate harmonisation of financial statements. Three Irish interviewees considered that the reports were too complicated for readers' understanding and one interviewee (IR3P) described them as 'almost unintelligible'. A UK preparer (UK1P) further asserted that even analysts did not understand the new accounting standards.

However, UK Big 4 auditor interviewee's (UK2A) auditing firm had undertaken research that discovered that some institutional investors had made different investment decisions about companies having seen their IFRS accounts for the first time. Importantly, he struggled to see why investment decisions would have altered on the basis of different standards and thought that these investors' reactions were likely to be from a misunderstanding of the information they had seen.

New reporting formats

On the new formats of the income statement and balance sheet, only the Italians (Panel F) thought that the new formats were more useful than their national GAAP predecessor. The majority of the UK (Panel E) and Irish (Panel G) interviewees disagreed that they were more useful. For example, the UK private investor's use of the disclosures in these accounts had not altered. He continued to head immediately to look at the change in the reported net asset figure:

If that increases you know its going well and if it's got brackets round it you know it's not going well.

In Italy, a Big 4 auditor (IT5A) noted that the new accounting formats would be of greater use to investors. He explained that, under Italian GAAP, creditors rather than investors were considered as the central stakeholder group to whom companies were required to report. This situation meant that Italian accounts had not reported figures of particular use to investors, such as earnings per share, which are now present in the newly formatted income statement. One Irish preparer (IR2P) claimed that IFRS had diminished the usefulness of financial statements and that the cash flow statement was the only remaining meaningful reporting tool because it had not been 'corrupted as much'.

Costs versus benefits

Overall, when asking whether the benefits had exceeded the costs there was a resounding 'no!' The costs were mainly attributable to the adaptation of information systems, training costs, consultation costs or the employment of individuals with specific IFRS knowledge who proved to be 'thin on the ground' and audit costs. The benefits were far more nebulous and thus there was agreement that overall the costs outweighed the benefits at present.

Comparability and international harmonisation

Most interviewees agreed that the benefits of greater transparency, comparability and uniformity would only materialise in the medium to long-term. One UK preparer (UK1P) suggested that any immediate opportunity to achieve these benefits was at present 'thwarted' by the number of options contained in IFRS.

Indeed, another preparer (UK6P) asserted that comparability would never be achieved while globally operating companies were required to satisfy the demands of two standards boards, the IASB and FASB. A UK preparer (UK5P) commented further that it would be interesting to see which of the two Boards' standards would be adopted in future by less developed economies such as India and China and acknowledged that: 'Political will is fundamental to getting these standards adopted and in place'.

Decision usefulness

In general, the UK and Irish interviewees did not think that reports compiled in accordance with IFRS would permit an improved analysis of a company's performance over an accounting period or any better predictive ability and hence did not assist decision-making. Only 3 of the 24 interviewees agreed that IFRS would assist decision making (Table 6.1). The Italian interviewees differed in this respect with seven out of eight agreeing; they all thought that the new standards, including the use of fair value measurements which had previously been prohibited under Italian GAAP, provided users with more forward-looking information, although one Italian user (IT6U) considered that it would only be the narrative disclosures rather than the financial statements themselves that would be useful in this regard. As Italian preparer (IT1P) commented:

> *...with IAS the users have more tools to assess future company performance trends and there is also more information, also of a strategic type.*

Conversely, a different Italian preparer (IR4P) commented that the combination of mark-to-market and historical costs in accounts was confusing for users and reduced their decision-usefulness. However, the

Italian interviewees referred to fair value methods as an improvement that would allow a company's 'hidden value to emerge' (IT2P).

Despite a need for some judgement to be applied when disclosing accounting information, the Italian users felt that increased comparability between sets of accounts would allow them to make better informed investment decisions. Italian preparer interviewee (IT4P) thought that reporting under IFRS made value-creation within a company much clearer than it had been previously in Italy and Italian preparer (IT3P) referred to specific standards, *IAS 8 Accounting Policies, Changes in Accounting Estimates and Errors* and *IAS 14 Segment Reporting*, as improving a user's ability to assess a company's performance as they effectively reduced accounting subjectivity. Another Italian preparer (IT1P) claimed that *IAS 36 Impairment of Assets* and *IFRS 3 Business Combinations*, provided users with more information that was previously only made available to analysts during company presentations.

However, not all Italians were so positive as one user (IT7U) argued:

> *IFRS entails greater volatility of profits and, consequently, of future cash flows due to the financial statement items assessed at fair value (e.g. stock options, financial instruments). This results in greater uncertainty of the assessment models, based on discounting back of the cash flows (DCF), and this situation cannot be completely overcome even by recourse to other assessment models.*

The UK and Irish interviewees had more reservations and a UK user (UK1U) did not think that IFRS statements would offer any more help to his investment decisions than reports prepared previously under UK GAAP. Private investor interviewee (UK3U) requested a change to financial reporting that was not part of IFRS: he requested that ratios should be calculated and shown on the face of the accounts to end the need for many investors to reach for their calculators when they received copies of annual reports.

The UK interviewees were more sceptical than their Italian counterparts because of the length and complexity of financial statements. For example, a UK preparer (UK3P) questioned:

> *I mean our annual report is how many pages? It's increased massively since last year there is an awful lot more disclosure and really you have to ask any ordinary investors are they really going to be any wiser?...people that are really interested get their information through other channels don't they?...*

An Irish preparer (IR3P) also noted:

> *The users of accounts- are they going to really understand what that's all about?... Following the letter of the law, but, without a doubt, the accounts are, I would say, significantly more difficult to understand.*

Summary

This chapter has built on the findings reported in chapter five by outlining some of the other implications of the introduction of IFRS in Europe. The findings show that the benefits do not appear to have outweighed the costs of implementing IFRS in the short term. Further, the importance of financial reporting to a company's reputation is only indirect, and any benefits of improved reporting only really accrue to capital markets participants. There is thought to be little effect on real cash flows, share prices, cost of capital or capital structure, so at present the companies themselves do not appear to benefit from cheaper financing for future investments. The effects of IFRS have been far more dramatic on the financial services sector, such as banks and insurers and the effect on mainland Europe, as evidenced by Italy, has been more far reaching than in the UK and Ireland. Most companies have only adopted IFRS for their consolidated accounts and have kept local GAAP for parent company and subsidiary accounts. This has been mainly for tax reasons and for dividend policy decisions. The interviewees thought that it is not yet possible to gauge the benefits of IFRS, that there is far too much choice within the standards and that comparability and harmonisation are still a long way off. Finally, the views of the Italian interviewees differed remarkably from the UK and Irish participants in this study; the Italians thought that financial statements were now more decision-useful – the UK and Irish did not. Thus the objective of the IASB for decision-useful financial information does not appear to have been met for the interviewees in this study.

The next chapter synthesises the findings from this chapter and the other three empirical chapters, presents policy implications and possibilities for future research.

7 Conclusions

Introduction

This report examines the implementation of IFRS in three countries, the UK, Italy and Ireland. A literature review is provided in chapter two, including an examination of the financial reporting cultures that exist in the UK, Italy and Ireland. Chapter three reviews the impact of IFRS on the disclosures and content of financial reports by examining the changes from the 2004 to 2005 annual reports. Chapter four examines the financial impact of IFRS from national GAAP on both income and net equity by analysing the disclosures in the reconciliation statements as mandated by *IFRS 1*. Chapters five and six report on interviews with preparers, auditors, users and regulators on how the implementation process was put into practice.

Content analysis

The results reported in chapter three demonstrate that the introduction of IFRS has had a significant effect on the reporting practices of the sampled companies in the UK, Italy and Ireland. In each of the three countries the disclosure expanded dramatically following the transition to IFRS. The change in disclosure was examined for seven categories of disclosure and breakdowns were provided by industry and market, where possible. In addition, the nature of the information provided was noted. Further analysis focused on identifying the standards that precipitated the most disclosure. In all three countries the derivatives standards occupied the greatest space in annual report disclosures. However, a difference was noted between countries in terms of the second most popular topic for disclosure; in the UK and Ireland considerable discussion of pensions-related matters took place, while the Italian documents focused on segmental reporting followed by pensions. It can be concluded, therefore, that the implementation of IFRS has had a significant and sizeable impact on the content of annual reports. The scale of this impact varies across companies and countries, with some companies supplying more information than others. The additional disclosure provided by the new reporting regime may have provided stakeholders with decision-useful information about these companies.

Reconciliation statements

The second strand of the empirical analysis examined the magnitude of the IFRS adjustments in the Reconciliation Statements of companies' reports as required by *IFRS 1*. This analysis initially expresses the income statement adjustments required by each standard as a percentage of the total profit (loss) and the balance sheet adjustments required by each Standard as a percentage of the total equity under national GAAP for all three countries. It then employs an index of Conservatism to study the size of the IFRS adjustments which companies reported in each of the three countries. The main conclusion from this second part of the empirical investigation is that, on average, IFRS adjustments increase the average reported profit figure of companies in all three countries, but reduce the IFRS equity figure in the balance sheet for the sample companies. However, variations in the impact of the balance sheet adjustments emerged for different countries. For example, the adjustments, on average, increased the reported equity figure in the balance sheets of Italian companies. In some cases, the percentage changes required by IFRS are sizeable. The index of Conservatism findings highlight that these adjustments are mainly due to a relatively small number of standards. For example, *IFRS 3 Business Combinations* (UK and Italy) and *IAS 40 Investment Property* (UK only), significantly increase the profit figure reported in the income statement under IFRS. This is countered by the negative impact of *IFRS 2 Share-based Payment* in Italy and Ireland. The standards that appear to have the largest impact and reduce the net equity figure under IFRS are *IAS 19 Employee Benefits* and *IAS 12 Income Taxes* (except Italy). *IFRS 2 Share-based Payment*, *IFRS 3 Business Combinations*, *IAS 10 Events after the Balance Sheet Date*, *IAS 16 Property, Plant and Equipment* and *IAS 38 Intangible Assets* result in an increase in the net equity figure in the balance sheet under IFRS. However, the index of Conservatism results suggest that the effect of IFRS is not common across the different nationalities of company included in the investigation; adjustments for IFRS are more pronounced for UK companies than for their Italian or Irish counterparts because of *IAS 40* and *IFRS 3*.

Findings from the interviews

Chapters five and six report on the findings from the interviews conducted with a number of parties who have been affected by the new reporting requirements of IFRS. The implementation process has been fairly similar in the three countries, although the Italian companies have tended to rely on their auditors more than the Irish or UK companies. Further, the Italian audit firms themselves often rely on their international technical offices which are based in London. Thus, the learning curve for Italian companies and auditors has probably been greater than for their UK and Irish counterparts.

The implementation process has been lengthy and audit firms started their process about five years before the implementation date of IFRS. Companies started their preparations on average two to three years before December 2005. One reason for this was the requirement for prior year comparatives, so companies had to prepare their opening balances sheets as at 1st January, 2004 on an IFRS basis.

The majority of companies set up project teams to implement the change, co-opting other people with specialist skills when necessary, especially treasury and pensions knowledge. The impact on companies' processes has varied depending upon their sector; financial institutions have had to do far more to implement IFRS than other sectors. Most companies have had to sort out specific accounting issues and disclosure requirements, but financial institutions often have had to change their whole processes and systems. The cost of implementation, thus, has varied enormously from virtually nothing to up to 100 million euros.

Some standards have caused far more difficulty to implement than others. *IAS 39 Financial Instruments* has been particularly difficult because, not only is the standard very lengthy, it is also very technically difficult, with derivatives coming on to the balance sheet for the first time and companies having to develop solutions to fair value all their derivative contracts. Further, if hedge accounting has been used, documentation has had to be put together to satisfy auditors that the hedge accounting rules have been satisfied.

Other standards that have also caused problems on implementation are *IAS 12*, *IAS 19*, *IAS 36*, *IAS 38*, *IFRS 2*, *IFRS 3* and *IFRS 8/IAS 14*. These are because the accounting is new and different (*IAS 19*), because preparers and auditors are unsure about the final requirements of a standard (*IAS 39/IFRS 8*), or because a lot of historical information has had to be gathered, such as on research and development and goodwill (*IAS 36*, *IAS 38*).

IFRS were introduced by the IASB to provide comparable information that is useful to users. The interviewees in this study do not think that IFRS has yet produced comparability, as there are too many choices available in the standards. For example, the Italian companies mostly choose the corridor approach under *IAS 19*, but UK and Irish companies generally choose the equity approach. Although most interviewees approve of accounting harmonisation, few want to go down this route if it means adopting the US rules-based approach. Further, interviewees from the UK and Ireland, in contrast to those from Italy, do not think that the financial statements are decision-useful as they are too long and too complex, often running to hundreds of pages. Indeed, most of the practitioners in this study do not think that the costs have been outweighed by the benefits. However, most think that in five years' time or so, comparability and usability might have improved.

Indeed, the Financial Reporting Council (FRC), in its Plan and Budget for 2008/09, highlighted that the recent credit market conditions mean that the risks to confidence in corporate reporting and governance are higher than they have been for a long time. In particular, it reminds market participants of:

> *The importance of disclosures relating to financing arrangements and risks and uncertainties in light of the credit market conditions and auditors' assessments of fair value and going concern.*

In the same document, the FRC states that one of its primary objectives is to ensure that the legislative and regulatory framework provides clarity in what is required to provide relevant, reliable, understandable and comparable reports and underpins the importance of a true and fair view. The legislative provisions in the EU (and hence IFRS) are a large component of this, but at present it is believed that the introduction of IFRS has been achieved without market disruption or loss of investor confidence. However, they recognise that there is a risk that the EU adopts EU IFRS rather than IASB IFRS, which in turn may make their financial statements incomparable with their peers abroad and might ultimately result in an increase in their cost of capital. The current research suggests that the comparability of financial statements of companies from different countries is not yet possible due to the variety of accounting choices available within IFRS. In its Plan and Budget for 2008/09, the FRC also acknowledges that:

> *The cumulative impact of legal and accounting requirements could result in the provision of information by companies in a form that is overly-complex and not sufficiently useful and relevant for users.*

The current research suggests that this might already be happening. Finally, the FRC notes that it intends to promote an appropriate degree of convergence between UK reporting standards and IFRS. In doing so, it comments that it would need 'to take into account the potential benefits and costs of convergence to both UK preparers and users'. The current research provides useful insights for the FRC in achieving that objective.

Policy implications and recommendations

From the findings of this study, either in the content analysis, analysis of the reconciliation statement or the interviews, a number of policy implications are suggested as follows:

- From the findings of the interviews and content analysis, annual reports have increased in size and now typically include more complex information. It is suggested that shorter, simpler annual reports that highlight management performance and that can be used as a basis for assessing the future prospects of companies may be helpful and could perhaps be considered by regulators and the IASB.
- The interviews indicated that enhanced comparability of financial reports would be beneficial. The choices of accounting treatments, for example in *IAS 19 Employee Benefits*, needs to be limited so that the performance of global companies operating on an international basis can be assessed by all stakeholders. The IASB should therefore continue to work towards this objective by limiting choices within standards.

- From the analysis of the reconciliation statement data, the large reduction in net equity for UK companies may have implications for companies wishing to raise additional finance if the strength of their balance sheets has been eroded, with higher gearing levels and greater perceptions of risk. This may prove especially so with the recent credit crunch. Maybe companies should communicate openly with external parties and ensure that stakeholders understand that the financial strength of their operations has not been affected by the change in financial reporting standards *per se*, although the changes may bring to light an issue or a situation that has not previously been disclosed or recognised.

- The interviewees identified that, all users, not just expert users, need to begin to understand IFRS to ensure that they do not apply misleading valuations to company securities. Additional training should be undertaken by institutional investors and analysts.

- From the content analysis and interviews the effect of IFRS was far greater for Italian companies and Italian users than for those based in the UK and Ireland. Language and cultural issues were factors in this difference. Perhaps the IASB and EU should ensure that translations are made available in a timely manner across all jurisdictions and made freely available on the IASB website. Additional funding of the IASB may therefore be required to facilitate this.

- The interviews highlighted that users need to engage more with the financial reporting process in order to understand and thus enhance the usability of financial reports and to ensure that published reports are useful for decision-making purposes. Perhaps more extensive communication and encouragement to engage in the IASB's consultation process would help in this regard.

- The interviewees also suggested that generic guidance should be produced to assist companies that are in the process of adopting IFRS about which standards to start with when planning the implementation of IFRS.

- From the interviews, it is suggested that audit firms and the professional bodies, such as ICAS, should be encouraged to produce joint documents advising on the interpretation and implementation of standards. Inconsistent advice between audit firms and belated advice have been confusing for preparers and users.

Summary

Overall, the implementation of IFRS has not been an easy process. Although the financial impact has often been negligible, the changes within organisations to their systems and processes should not be under-estimated. Hopefully these policy recommendations will be considered and progressed and that this will assist companies adopting IFRS in the future so that they will find the process much easier.

REFERENCES

Abd-Elsalam, O.H. and Weetman, P., (2003) 'Introducing International Accounting Standards to an emerging capital market: relative familiarity and language effect in Egypt', *Journal of International Accounting, Auditing and Taxation*, Vol. 12, pp. 63-84.

Adams, C. and Harte, G. (1998), 'Making Discrimination Visible: The Potential for Social Accounting', *Accounting Forum*, March, Vol. 24, No. 1, pp. 56-79.

Aisbitt, S. (2006), 'Assessing the effect of the transition to IFRS on equity: the case of the FTSE 100', *Accounting in Europe*, Vol. 3, pp. 117-133.

Appleyard, A. and Strong, N. (1984), 'The Impact of *SSAP 16* Current Cost Accounting Disclosures on Security Prices', in *Current Cost Accounting: The Benefits and Costs*, Institute of Chartered Accountants in England and Wales, London.

Arnold, J. and Moizer, P. (1984), 'A Survey of the Methods used by UK Investment Analysts to Appraise Investments in Ordinary Shares', *Accounting and Business Research*, Summer, pp. 195-207.

Auer, K.V., (1996), 'Capital market reactions to earnings announcements: empirical evidence on the difference in the information content of IAS-based earnings and EU-Directives-based earnings', *The European Accounting Review*, Vol. 5, No. 4, pp. 587-623.

Balakrishnan, R., Harris, T. and Sen, P.K. (1990), 'The Predictive Ability of Geographic Segment Disclosures', *Journal of Accounting Research,* Vol. 28, No.2, pp. 305-325.

Beattie, V. and Pratt, K. (2001), *Business Reporting: Harnessing the Power of the Internet for Users*, Edinburgh: Institute of Chartered Accountants of Scotland.

Beattie, V. and Pratt, K. (2003), 'Issues Concerning Web-Based Business Reporting: An Analysis of the views of Interested Parties', *British Accounting Review,* Vol. 35, pp. 155-187.

Beaver, W., Lambert, R. and Morse, D. (1980), 'The Information Content of Security Prices', *Journal of Accounting and Economics*, Vol. 1, pp. 3-28.

Belkaoui, A. (2004), *Accounting Theory*, Thomson, Padstow.

Bonham M., Curtis M., Davies M., Dekker P., Denton T., Moore R., Richards H., Wilkinson-Riddle G. and Wilson A., (2004), *International GAAP (2005)*, LexisNexis, London.

Brown, P. and Tarca, A., (2005), 'A commentary on issues relating to the enforcement of International Financial Reporting Standards in the EU', *European Accounting Review*, Vol. 14, No. 1, pp. 181-212.

Buchanan, F.R. (2003), 'International Accounting Harmonisation: Developing a Single World Standard', *Business Horizons*, May-June, pp. 61-70.

Bush, T. (2005), *Divided by a common language: Where economics meets the law: USsus non-US financial reporting models*, ICAEW, London, 58 pp.

Cairns, D. (2004), 'The implications of IAS/IFRS for UK companies', *International Journal of Disclosure and Governance,* Vol. 1, No. 2, pp. 107-118.

Canibãno, L. and Mora, A. (2000), 'Evaluating the Statistical Significance of 'de facto' Accounting Harmonization: A Study of European Global Players', *The European Accounting Review*, vol.9, n.3.

Carsberg, B. and Day, J. (1984), 'The Use of Current Cost Accounting Information by Stockbrokers', in *Current Cost Accounting: The Benefits and Costs*, Institute of Chartered Accountants in England and Wales, London.

Chambers, R. (1955), 'Blueprint for a Theory of Accounting', Accounting Research, January, pp. 17-25.

Collins, D. (1975), 'SEC Product Line Reporting and Market Efficiency', *Journal of Financial Economics*, June, pp. 125-164.

Crawford, L., Dunne, T., Hannah, G. and Stevenson, L. (2008), *An exploration of Scottish charities' governance and accountability*, ICAS, Edinburgh.

Cuijpers, R. and Buijink, W., (2005), ' Voluntary adoption of non-local GAAP in the European Union: a study of determinants and consequences', *European Accounting Review*, Vol. 14, No. 3, pp. 487-524.

Cyert, R. and Ijiri, Y. (1974), 'Problems of Implementing the Trueblood Objectives Report', *Journal of Accounting Research (Supplement)*, pp. 29-45.

Darenidou, C. McLeay, S. and Raonic, I. (2006), 'Expected earnings growth and the cost of capital: An analysis of accounting regime change in the European financial market', *Abacus*, Vol. 42, Nos.3/4, pp. 388-414.

Daske (2006), 'Economic Benefits of Adopting IFRS or US-GAAP – Have the Expected Cost of Equity Capital Really Decreased?', *Journal of Business, Finance and Accounting*, Vol.33, Nos. 3/4, pp.329-373.

Daske, H. and Gebhardt, G. (2006), 'International Financial Reporting Standards and experts perceptions of disclosure quality', *Abacus,* Vol. 42, Nos.3/4, pp. 461-498.

De Berg, C. and Shriver, K. (1987), 'The Relevance of Current Cost Accounting Data', *Journal of Accounting Literature*, Vol. 6, pp. 55-87.

Delvaille, P. Ebbers, G. and Saccon, C. (2005), 'International Financial reporting convergence: Evidence from three continental European countries', *Accounting in Europe*, Vol. 2, pp.137-164.

Dey, C. (1999), 'Social Accounting and Accountability: Ethnography, Bookkeeping and the Critical Project', Unpublished PhD, University of Dundee.

Dumontier, P. and Raffournier, B., (1998), 'Why firms comply voluntarily with IAS: an empirical analysis with Swiss data', *Journal of International Financial Management and Accounting,* Vol. 9, No. 3, pp.216-245.

Dunne, T. M., Helliar, C.V., Mallin, C.A., Moir,L., Ow-Yong,K. and Power, D.M. (2003), *The Financial Reporting of Derivatives and Other Financial Instruments: A Study of the Implementation and Disclosures of FRS 13,* Research Report, Institute of Chartered Accountants in England and Wales, London.

Dunne, T. M., Helliar, C. V., Power, D. M., Mallin, C. A. Ow-Yong, K. and Moir, L. (2004), 'The Introduction of Derivatives Reporting in the UK: A Content Analysis of FRS 13 Disclosures', *The Journal of Derivatives Accounting,* Vol. 1, No. 2, September, pp. 205-219.

Edwards, P. and Smith, R. (1996), 'Competitive Disadvantage and Voluntary Disclosures: The Case of Segmental Reporting', *British Accounting Review*, Vol. 28, pp. 155-172.

El-Gazzar, S. M., Finn, P. M. and Jacob, R. (1999), 'An empirical investigation of multinational firms' compliance with International Accounting Standards', *The International Journal of Accounting,* Vol. 34, No. 2, pp. 239-248.

Emenyonu, E. and Gray, S. (1992), 'EC Accounting Harmonisation: An Empirical Study of Measurement Practices in France, Germany and the UK', *Accounting and Business Research*, Vol. 23, No. 89, Winter, pp. 49-58.

Ernst & Young (2006), IFRS: Observations on the implementation of IFRS, Sept, E&Y, London, pp30.

Financial Accounting Standards Board (1978), *Statement of Financial Accounting Concepts No. 1: Objectives of Financial Reporting by Business Enterprises,* FASB.

Fearnley, S. and Hines, T. (2002), 'The Adoption of International Accounting Standards in the UK: A Review of Attitudes', Working Paper, Portsmouth Business School.

Fearnley, S. Gillies, A. Hines, T. and Willett, C. (2007), '*Bewildered but better informed: A qualitative interview based study into the attitudes of some UK accountants and regulators to the EU IFRS conversion project prior to its implementation in the UK*', London, ICAEW, 103pp.

Financial Reporting Council (2008) Plan and Budget for 2008/09, London.

Fox, A.M., Dunne, T.M. and Helliar, C.V. (2007), 'The governance of pension funds: an investigation', Paper presented at the BAA corporate Governance Special Interest Group, Royal Holloway, London.

Goodwin, J. and Ahmed, K. (2006), 'The impact of international financial reporting standards: Does size matter?', *Managerial Auditing Journal*, Vol. 21, No. 5, pp. 460-475.

Govindarajan, G. (1980), 'The Objectives of Financial Statements: An Empirical Study of the Use of Cash Flow and Earnings by Security Analysts', *Accounting, Organisations and Society*, Vol. 5, pp. 383-392.

Gray, S J (1980): 'The Impact of International Accounting Differences from a Security-Analysis Perspective: Some European Evidence', *Journal of Accounting Research*, Vol. 18, No. 1, pp. 64-76.

Gray, R.H., Kouhy, K. and Lavers, S. (1995), 'Constructing a Research Database of Social and Environmental Reporting by UK Companies: A Methodological Note', *Accounting, Auditing and Accountability Journal,* Vol. 8, No 2, pp. 78-101.

Haller, A. (2002), 'Financial Accounting Developments in the European Union: Past Events and Future Prospects', *The European Accounting Review*, Vol. 11, No. 1 pp. 153-190.

Haverals, J. (2007), 'IAS/IFRS in Belgium: Quantitative analysis of the impact on the tax burden of companies', *Journal of International Accounting, Auditing and Taxation,* Vol. 16, pp. 68-89.

Institute of Chartered Accountants in England and Wales (1975), *The Corporate Report,* London: ICAEW.

Institute of Chartered Accountants in England and Wales (2006), *Disclosure responsibilities and building trust and promoting transparent and reliable information*, July, London: ICAEW, 34pp.

Institute of Chartered Accountants in England and Wales (2007), *EU implementation of IFRS and the fair value directive: A report for the European Commission*, October, London, 251pp.

Institute of Chartered Accountants of Scotland (2006), *Principles not Rules: A Question of Judgement*, Edinburgh: ICAS.

Institute of Chartered Accountants of Scotland (2007a), *Principles into Practice: Key points from the too late for principles? Conference held in October 2006*, February, Edinburgh, ICAS, 19pp.

Institute of Chartered Accountants of Scotland (2007b), *Principles into Practice: Key points from the New York Conference April 2007*, June, Edinburgh, ICAS, 23pp.

International Accounting Standards Committee (1989), *Framework for the Preparation and Presentation of Financial Statements,* London, IASC.

International Accounting Standards Board (2006), *Preliminary View on an improved Conceptual Framework for Financial Reporting: The Objective of Financial Reporting and Qualitative Characteristics of Decision-useful Financial Reporting Information*, Discussion paper, July 2006.

Jaggi, B. and Low, P.K., (2000), 'Impact of culture, market forces, and legal system on financial disclosures', *International Journal of Accounting,* Vol. 35, No. 4, pp.495-519.

Jermakowicz, E.K. and Gornik-Tomaszewski, S. (2006), 'Implementing IFRS from the perspective of EU publicly traded companies', *Journal of International Accounting, Auditing and Taxation*, Vol. 15, pp.170-196.

Jones, D and Cunningham, T. (2003) 'Closed DB Schemes: A new Strategy' *The Treasurer*, November.

Jones, M. and Shoemaker, P. (1994), 'Accounting Narratives: A Review of Empirical Studies of Content and Readability', *Journal of Accounting Literature,* Vol. 13, pp.142-184.

Joshi, P.L. and Ramadhan, S., (2002), 'The adoption of international accounting standards by small and closely held companies: evidence from Bahrain', *International Journal of Accounting*, Vol. 37, pp. 429-440.

KPMG (2006), 'The application of IFRS: Choices in practice', KPMG, London, 36pp.

KPMG (2007), *International Financial Reporting Standards: The quest for a global language,* London, KPMG, 46pp.

Krippendorff, K (1980), *Content Analysis: An Introduction to its Methodology,* Sage, New York.

Krippendorf, K. (2003), *Content Analysis: An Introduction to its Methodology,* New York: Sage.

La Porta, R., Lopez-de-Silanes, F., Schleifer,A. and Vishny, R. (1998), 'Law and Finance', *Journal of Political Economy*, Vol. 106, pp. 1113-1155.

Larson, R.K. and Street, D.L. (2004), 'Convergence with IFRS in an Expanding Europe: Progress and Obstacles Identified by Large Accounting Firms' Survey', *Journal of International Accounting, Auditing and Taxation*, Vol. 13, pp. 89-119.

Lee, T. and Tweedie, D. (1979), 'The Private Shareholder and the Corporate Report', London: Institute of Chartered Accountants in England and Wales.

Mallin, C. (1999), 'Financial institutions and their relations with corporate boards', *Corporate Governance: An international review*, Vol. 7, pp. 248-255.

Marchi, L. (ed.) (2000), *L'applicazione dei principi contabili nei bilanci delle imprese,* Il Sole 24 Ore, Milan.

McLeay, S. (2006), '*Forum: International Financial Reporting*', Abacus, Vol. 42, Nos. ¾, pp. 291-295.

Meek, G. and Saudagaran, S. (1990), 'A survey of research on financial reporting in a transitional context', *Journal of Accounting Literature*, p.150.

Milne, M. and Adler, R. (1999), 'Exploring the Reliability of Social and Environmental Disclosures Content Analysis', *Accounting, Auditing and Accountability Journal*, Vol. 12(2), pp.237-256.

Pirinen, P., (2005), 'Economic and normative pressures as drivers for the adoption of International Accounting Standards in Finland since 1976', *European Accounting Review*, Vol. 14, No. 1, pp.213-235.

Prather-Kinsey, J. and Meek, G. K. (2004), 'The Effect of Revised *IAS 14* on Segment Reporting by IAS Companies', *European Accounting Review*, Vol. 13, No. 2, pp. 213-234.

PriceWaterhouseCoopers (2005), *The investors' view,* November, London, PWC, pp. 8.

PriceWaterhouseCoopers (2006a), *IFRS: Embracing Change*, July, London, PWC, 27pp.

PriceWaterhouseCoopers (2006b), *IFRS and the impact on tax for the retail sector*, PWC, London, 4pp.

PriceWaterhouseCoopers (2006c), *IFRS and AIM: How ready are you?*, November, PWC, London, 17pp.

PriceWaterhouseCoopers (2006d), *Reporting under the new regime: A survey of 2005 IFRS insurance annual reports,* July, PWC, London, 32pp.

PriceWaterhouseCoopers (2006e), IFRS: The European Investors' view, February, PWC, London, 9pp.

PriceWaterhouseCoopers (2007), IFRS and its impact on financial reporting for the life sciences sector, January, PWC, London, 18pp.

Pro-active accounting activities in Europe: PAAinE (2007), *Stewardship/accountability as an objective of financial reporting: a comment on the IASB/FASB conceptual framework project*, Accounting Standards Board, Foreningen af Statsatoriserede revisor, Deutches Rechnungslegungs Standards Committee, Komitet Standardow Rachunklow-ci and EFRAG, June, 18pp.

Richer, J. and Sellhorn, T., (2005), 'Do harmonized accounting standards achieve harmonized accounting practices? – evidence from China', paper presented at EAA Conference, Gothenburg, March.

Salvioni, D. (1992), *Il bilancio d'esercizio nella comunicazione integrate d'impresa*, Giappichelli, Turin.

Schultz, J. and Lopez, T. (2001), 'The impact of national influence on accounting estimates: implications for international accounting standard-setters', *The International Journal of Accounting*, Vol. 36, pp.271-290.

Sellhorn, T. and Gornik-Tomaszewski, S. (2006), 'Implications of the IAS Regulation for research into the international differences in accounting systems', *Accounting in Europe*, Vol. 3, pp. 187-217.

Sterling, R. (1972), 'Decision-Orientated Financial Accounting', *Accounting and Business Research*, Summer, pp. 198-208.

Street, D. L. (2002), 'An interview with Sir David Tweedie', *Journal of International Financial Management and Accounting*, Vol. 13, No. 1, pp. 73-100.

Street, D.L. (2006), 'The G4's role in the evolution of the international accounting standard setting process and the partnership with the IASB', *Journal of International Accounting, Auditing and Taxation*, Vol. 15, pp. 109-126.

Street, D. L. and Bryant, S. M. (2000), 'Disclosure Level and Compliance with IASs: A Comparison of Companies With and Without U.S. Listings and Filings', *The International Journal of Accounting*, Vol. 35, No. 3 pp. 305-329.

Street, D. L. and Gray, S. J. (2002), 'Factors Influencing the Extent of Corporate Compliance with International Accounting Standards: Summary of a Research Monograph', *Journal of International Accounting, Auditing and Taxation*, Vol. 11, pp. 51-76.

Street, D. L., Gray, S. J. and Bryant, S. M. (1999), 'Acceptance and observance of International Accounting Standards: an empirical study of companies claiming to comply with IASs', *The International Journal of Accounting*, Vol. 34, No. 1, pp.11-48.

Street, D. L., Nichols, N.B. and Gray, S. J. (2000), 'Assessing the Acceptability of International Accounting Standards in the US: An Empirical Study of the Materiality of US GAAP Reconciliations by Non-US Companies Complying with IASC Standards', *The International Journal of Accounting*, Vol. 35, No. 1 pp. 27-63.

Street, D. L. and Shaughnessy, K. A. (1998), 'The Quest for International Accounting Harmonization: A Review of the Standard Setting Agendas of the IASC, US, UK, Canada and Australia, 1973-1997', *The International Journal of Accounting*, Vol. 33, No. 2, pp. 179-209.

Tarca, A. (2004), 'International Convergence of Accounting Practices: Choosing Between IAS and US GAAP', *Journal of International Financial Management and Accounting*, Vol. 15, No. 1, pp. 60-91.

Taylor, M. E. and Jones, R. A. (1999), 'The Use of International Accounting Standards Terminology, A Survey of IAS Compliance Disclosure', *The International Journal of Accounting*, Vol. 34, No. 4, pp. 557-570.

Teodori, C. (ed.) (2006), *L'adozione degli IAS/IFRS in Italia: le attività immateriali e l'impairement test*, Giappichelli, Turin.

Tilt, C A (1997), 'Environmental Policies of Major Companies: Australian Evidence', *British Accounting Review*, Vol. 29(4), pp.367-394.

Unerman, J (2000), 'Methodological Issues: Reflections on Quantification in Corporate Social Reporting Content Analysis', *Accounting, Auditing and Accountability Journal*, Vol. 13(5), pp.667-680.

Van Tendeloo, B. and Vanstraelen, A. (2005), 'Earnings management under German GAAP versus IFRS, *European Accounting Review*, Vol. 14, No. 1, pp. 155-180.

Weber, R P (1985), *Basic Content Analysis*, Sage Publications, Beverly Hills.

Weetman, P. and Gray, S. (1990), 'International Financial Analysis and Comparative Corporate Performance: The Impact of UK Versus US Accounting Principles on Earnings', *Journal of International Financial Management and Accounting*, Vol. 21, No. 2/3, pp. 111-129.

Weetman, P. and Gray, S. (1991), 'A Comparative International Analysis of the Impact of Accounting Principles on Profits: The USA Versus the UK, Sweden and the Netherlands', *Accounting and Business Research*, Vol. 21, No. 84, pp. 363-379.

Weetman, P, Jones E., Adams,C. and Gray, S. (1998), 'Profit Measurement and UK Accounting Standards: A Case of Increasing Disharmony in Relation to US GAAP and IASs', *Accounting and Business Research*, Vol. 28, No. 3, pp. 189-203.

World Federation of Exchanges (2008), *Annual Report & Statistics 2007,* World Federation of Exchanges, 30th May, 2008.

Zeff, S. A. (1999), 'The coming confrontation on International Accounting Standards, *Irish Accounting Review,* Vol. 5, No. 2, pp.89-117.

Zeff, S.A. (2007) 'Some obstacles to global financial reporting comparability and convergence at a high level of quality, *British accounting Review*, Vol. 39, pp. 290-302.

APPENDIX A

CONTENT ANALYSIS - SAMPLE COMPANIES

Table A.1 UK sample

Company	SE Listing	Industry
3i	FTSE100	Financials
Acal	FTSEOther	Industrials
Albion (Hardy Underwriting Group)	FTSEOther	Consumer Goods
Alliance Unichem	FTSE100	Health Care
Amstrad	FTSEOther	Consumer Goods
Amvescap	FTSE100	Financials
Anglo American	FTSE100	Basic Materials
Antofagasta	FTSE100	Basic Materials
Associated British Foods	FTSE100	Consumer Goods
Aston Villa	FTSEOther	Consumer Services
AstraZeneca	FTSE100	Health Care
Aviva	FTSE100	Financials
AWG	FTSEOther	Utilities
BAA	FTSE100	Industrials
BAE Systems	FTSE100	Industrials
Barclays	FTSE100	Financials
Beale	FTSEOther	Consumer Services
Bespak	FTSEOther	Health Care
BG Group	FTSE100	Oil & Gas
BHP Billiton	FTSE100	Basic Materials
Body Shop International	FTSEOther	Consumer Services
Boots Group	FTSE100	Consumer Services
BP	FTSE100	Oil & Gas
Brammer	FTSEOther	Industrials
British Airways	FTSE100	Consumer Services
British American Tobacco	FTSE100	Consumer Goods
British Land Co	FTSE100	Financials
British Sky Broadcasting Group	FTSE100	Consumer Services
BT Group	FTSE100	Telecommunications
Cable & Wireless	FTSE100	Telecommunications
Cadbury Schweppes	FTSE100	Consumer Goods
Caffe Nero Group	FTSEOther	Consumer Services
Capita Group	FTSE100	Industrials
Care UK	FTSEOther	Health Care
Centrica	FTSE100	Oil & Gas
Chapelthorpe	FTSEOther	Consumer Goods
Christie Group	FTSEOther	Industrials
CML Microsystems	FTSEOther	Technology
Compass Group	FTSE100	Industrials
Corin Group	FTSEOther	Health Care
Daily Mail & General Trust	FTSE100	Consumer Services
Diageo	FTSE100	Consumer Goods
Dixons Group	FTSE100	Consumer Services

Table A.1 UK sample (cont.)

Company	SE Listing	Industry
Domino Printing Sciences	FTSEOther	Industrials
Elementis	FTSEOther	Basic Materials
EMAP	FTSE100	Consumer Services
Enterprise Inns	FTSE100	Consumer Services
Flying Brands	FTSEOther	Consumer Services
Friends Provident	FTSE100	Financials
Gallaher Group	FTSE100	Consumer Goods
Game Group	FTSEOther	Consumer Services
GlaxoSmithkline	FTSE100	Health Care
Gleeson (M.J.) Group	FTSEOther	Industrials
Great Portland Estates	FTSEOther	Financials
GUS	FTSE100	Consumer Services
Hammerson	FTSE100	Financials
Hampson Industries	FTSEOther	Industrials
Hanson	FTSE100	Industrials
Hays	FTSE100	Industrials
HBOS	FTSE100	Financials
Helphire Group	FTSEOther	Financials
HSBC Hldgs	FTSE100	Financials
Huntleigh Technology	FTSEOther	Health Care
IMI	FTSEOther	Industrials
Imperial Chemical Industries	FTSE100	Basic Materials
Imperial Tobacco Group	FTSE100	Consumer Goods
Intercontinental Hotels Group	FTSE100	Consumer Services
Intermediate Capital Group	FTSEOther	Financials
International Power	FTSE100	Utilities
Johnson Matthey	FTSE100	Basic Materials
Johnston Press	FTSEOther	Consumer Services
Kingfisher	FTSE100	Consumer Services
Kingston Communications	FTSEOther	Telecommunications
Land Securities Group	FTSE100	Financials
Legal & General Group	FTSE100	Financials
Liberty International	FTSE100	Financials
Lincat Group	FTSEOther	Industrials
Lloyds TSB Group	FTSE100	Financials
London Stock Exchange	FTSEOther	Financials
Man Group	FTSE100	Financials
Marks & Spencer Group	FTSE100	Consumer Services
Matalan	FTSEOther	Consumer Services
Morrison (Wm.) Supermarkets	FTSE100	Consumer Services
Morse	FTSEOther	Technology
National Grid Transco	FTSE100	Utilities
Next	FTSE100	Consumer Services
Northern Rock	FTSE100	Financials
NSB Retail Systems	FTSEOther	Technology
Old Mutual	FTSE100	Financials
Paragon Group Of Companies	FTSEOther	Financials
Pearson	FTSE100	Consumer Services
Pennon Group	FTSEOther	Utilities
Plasmon	FTSEOther	Technology

Table A.1 UK sample (cont.)

Company	SE Listing	Industry
Prudential	FTSE100	Financials
R.E.A.Hldgs	FTSEOther	Consumer Goods
Reckitt Benckiser	FTSE100	Consumer Goods
Reed Elsevier	FTSE100	Consumer Services
Regus Group	FTSEOther	Industrials
Rentokil Initial	FTSE100	Industrials
Reuters Group	FTSE100	Consumer Services
Rexam	FTSE100	Industrials
Rio Tinto	FTSE100	Basic Materials
Rolls Royce Group	FTSE100	Industrials
Royal & Sun Alliance Insurance Group	FTSE100	Financials
Royal Bank Of Scotland Group	FTSE100	Financials
RPC Group	FTSEOther	Industrials
SABMiller	FTSE100	Consumer Goods
Sage Group	FTSE100	Technology
Sainsbury (J)	FTSE100	Consumer Services
Schroders	FTSE100	Financials
Scottish & Newcastle	FTSE100	Consumer Goods
Scottish & Southern Energy	FTSE100	Utilities
Scottish Power	FTSE100	Utilities
Severn Trent	FTSE100	Utilities
Shell Transport & Trading Co	FTSE100	Oil & Gas
Shire Pharmaceuticals Group	FTSE100	Health Care
Skyepharma	FTSEOther	Health Care
Smith & Nephew	FTSE100	Health Care
Smiths Group	FTSE100	Industrials
Spring Group	FTSEOther	Industrials
Standard Chartered	FTSE100	Financials
Tate & Lyle	FTSE100	Consumer Goods
Taylor Nelson Sofres	FTSEOther	Consumer Services
Telspec	FTSEOther	Telecommunications
Tesco	FTSE100	Consumer Services
Topps Tiles	FTSEOther	Consumer Services
Tribal Group	FTSEOther	Industrials
Unilever	FTSE100	Consumer Goods
United Utilities	FTSE100	Utilities
Vodafone Group	FTSE100	Telecommunications
Volex Group	FTSEOther	Industrials
Weir Group	FTSEOther	Industrials
Whitbread	FTSE100	Consumer Services
Wolseley	FTSE100	Industrials
Woolworths Group	FTSEOther	Consumer Services
WPP Group	FTSE100	Consumer Services
Xstrata	FTSE100	Basic Materials
Yell Group	FTSE100	Consumer Services

Note: Table A.1 provides basic details relating to the UK sampled companies. Details pertaining to industry sector were based on the Industry Classification Benchmark (ICB) categorisation. FTSE Other companies are a random sample of FTSE All Share Index listed companies outside the FTSE 100.

Table A.2 Italy sample

Company	Industry
Alleanza Assicurazioni	Financials
Autostrade	Industrials
Banca Nazionale del Lavoro (BNL)	Financials
Banche Popolari Unite (BPU)	Financials
Banca Antonveneta	Financials
Banca Fideuram	Financials
Banca Intesa	Financials
Banca Monte dei Paschi di Siena (MPS)	Financials
Banco Popolare di Verona e Novara (VReNO)	Financials
Capitalia	Financials
Edison	Utilities
Enel	Utilities
Eni	Oil & Gas
Fiat	Consumer Goods
Finmeccanica	Industrials
Generali Assicurazioni	Financials
Mediaset S.P.A.	Consumer Services
Mediobanca	Financials
Mediolanum	Financials
Ras	Financials
Saipem	Industrials
San Paolo Imi	Financials
Seat Pagine Gialle	Consumer Services
Snam Rete Gas	Utilities
Telecom Italia	Telecommunications
Terna	Utilities
Unicredito	Financials

Note: Table A.2 provides basic details relating to the Italian sampled companies. All are listed on the MIB 30. Details pertaining to industry sector were based on the Industry Classification Benchmark (ICB) categorisation.

Table A.3 Ireland sample

Company	Industry
Allied Irish Bank	Financials
Bank Of Ireland	Financials
C R H	Industrials
DCC	Industrials
Eircom Group	Telecommunications
Elan Corporation	Health Care
F B D Holdings	Financials
Glanbia	Consumer Goods
IAWS Group	Consumer Goods
Kerry Group	Consumer Goods

Note: Table A.3 provides basic details relating to the Irish sampled companies. All are listed on the ISEQ. Details pertaining to industry sector were based on the Industry Classification Benchmark (ICB) categorisation.

APPENDIX B

CONTENT ANALYSIS DECISION RULES

General

The content analysis sample was drawn from companies listed in three countries. In the UK the FTSE 100 and a random sample of other companies listed on the LSE were used. The Italian sample was based on the MIB30, while the Irish sample was based on a random sample of ISEQ-listed companies. The content analysis is based on methodologies previously adopted in other studies, in particular, those employed by Gray *et al.* (1995); Dunne *et al.* (2003; 2004) and Crawford *et al.* (2007).

Unit of measurement

- A standard A4 template divided into percentages of a page, with a standard margin; measures proportions of page.
- Margins and blank areas of pages are to be associated with words, tables etc. covering the areas of disclosure.
- Actual physical size of page is to be ignored.

Evidence category

- Disclosures may be either narrative (N) or numerical (Q) in nature.

Auditable/verifiable

Disclosure is categorised as 'auditable' if, given access to the organisation, it would be possible to confirm the statements made.

News

- Good – statements beyond the minimum which include, for example, specific details where these details have a creditable or neutral reflection on the company; any statements which reflect credit on the company; upbeat analysis/discussion/ statements.
- Neutral – statement of policy or intent within statutory minimum with no details of what or how; statement of fact whose credit/ discredit to the company is not obvious – which are unaccompanied by editorialising.
- Bad – any statement which reflects/might reflect discredit on the company.

Location in annual report

Possible locations include: Chairman's Statement; Financial Director's Review; Chief Executive's Review; Operating and Financial Review; Directors' Report; Corporate Governance Statement; Remuneration Report; Accounting Policies; Notes to the Accounts; IFRS Compliance Statement; Statement of Directors' Responsibilities; Other

Memo

- For any additional information or disclosure of particular note.

Categories of disclosure

The principal content analysis classification categories were based on a review of the extant professional and academic literature. A breakdown of the items expected under each of the headings is provided in these decision rules.

1. Factual information

Information concerning the harmonisation process and the implementation of IFRS. Also includes information that outlines where users can find IAS/IFRS data in the financial report.

Examples:

- European Regulation no. 1606/2002 states that...
- The first financial statement that will be prepared according to IFRS will be ...
- This is the first financial report that is prepared according to IFRS and the criteria adopted are the same as those that will be used for preparation of the consolidated...
- The final section of the appendix contains information about the effects of the IAS/IFRS...
- For more information about the impacts of the IAS/IFRS reference is made to the specific section of the Appendix...

2. Cost of implementation

This category deals with details regarding the cost of implementation of the IFRS reporting regime. The information must be very specific.

Example:

- Company has spent over £150m on complying with new regulations…

3. General impact of implementation

Information concerning the general impact/implications of implementation of the IFRS reporting regime. The information could be positive/negative/neutral in orientation. The information could relate to general problems associated with implementation of IAS/IFRS. Finally, the information could relate to the general impact of the IAS/IFRS on the financial performance of the company.

Examples:

- IFRS will improve financial communication and will have a positive impact on the users in making decisions because…
- IFRS will have a negative impact on the users in making decisions because…
- IFRS will not improve financial communication and will not have any impact on the users in making decisions because…
- The implementation of IFRS could cause these problems… because…
- The general impact associated with the implementation of IAS/IFRS is an increase in the equity equal to £250 million.

4. Progress to date

Information concerning the transition process phase.

Examples:

- To facilitate this transition a project has been initiated…
- In the short term, the project for the implementation of the IFRS seeks to quantify accounting entries in accordance with the timetable for the introduction of the international standards…
- The program for the implementation of the IAS/IFRS can be divided into two phases. In the first phase the Group has organised specific training courses, in the second phase…

5. Operational & strategic decisions taken by management

Information about specific operational and strategic decisions taken by managers owing to the implementation of IAS/IFRS.

Example:

- Before the implementation of IAS/IFRS the Group decided to sell two subsidiaries because…

6. Implementation & Impact of Individual Standards

This information must be related specifically to the Group. There are two principal types of information: (i) information about the application of individual IAS/IFRS; and (ii) information about the effects of the application of individual IAS/IFRS.

This category will be totalled for inclusion in the main analysis. However, a breakdown by standard will also be included.

7. General Other

- any other relevant disclosures.

APPENDIX C

CONTENT ANALYSIS TEMPLATE

IFRS Content Analysis Template							
Company name							
Year 1/2 1/4 2/4 3/4 4/4 y/e (circle as appropriate)							
(Interim/Qtrly only) Audited: Yes/No Independent Review Report: Yes/No							
Total pages/accountancy pages							
Category	Prop. of Page	Evidence	Auditable	News	Location	Page no.	Memo
Factual information							
Cost of implementation							
General impact of implementation							
Progress to date							
Operational & strategic decisions taken by mgt.							
Implementation & Impact of individual standards							
General other							
TOTAL							

APPENDIX D

CONTENT ANALYSIS - EXTRA TABLES

Table D.1 UK sample – Analysis by market (percentage of annual report devoted to IFRS disclosure)

Panel A – FTSE 100

Type of disclosure	Pre IFRS	Post IFRS	Diff	P-Value
Factual information	0.3076	0.6684	0.3608	0.0000
Cost of implementation	0.0095	0.0129	0.0034	0.2610
General impact of implementation	0.1201	0.3064	0.1863	0.0000
Progress to date	0.0661	0.0220	-0.0441	0.0000
Operational & strategic decisions taken by management	0.0134	0.0053	-0.0081	0.2710
Implementation and impact of individual standards	1.1910	8.7460	7.5550	0.0000
General other	0.0000	0.0087	0.0087	-
TOTAL	1.7070	9.7700	8.0630	0.0000

Panel B – FTSE other

Type of disclosure	Pre IFRS	Post IFRS	Diff	P-Value
Factual information	0.2287	1.1655	0.9368	0.0000
Cost of implementation	0.0009	0.0120	0.0111	0.0090
General impact of implementation	0.1017	0.2548	0.1531	0.0020
Progress to date	0.0959	0.0144	-0.0815	0.0010
Operational & strategic decisions taken by management	0.0011	0.0006	-0.0005	0.6690
Implementation and impact of individual standards	0.5650	8.4700	7.9050	0.0000
General other	0.0000	0.0003	0.0003	-
TOTAL	0.9930	9.9180	8.9250	0.0000

Notes: This table shows the IFRS information provided by UK companies by market listing. This information is based on the percentage of the annual report devoted to IFRS-related information reported by companies across the seven disclosure categories. Panel A presents this information for companies listed on the FTSE 100 market, while Panel B details this information for FTSE Other companies. The mean p-values are based on a 2-sample t-test.

Table D.2 UK sample – Narrative versus numerical (percentage of annual report devoted to IFRS disclosures)

Panel A – Narrative

Type of disclosure	Pre IFRS	Post IFRS	Diff	P-Value
Factual information	0.2774	0.8413	0.5639	0.0000
Cost of implementation	0.0051	0.0037	-0.0014	0.3350
General impact of implementation	0.0780	0.1280	0.0500	0.0000
Progress to date	0.0764	0.0193	-0.0571	0.0000
Operational & strategic decisions taken by management	0.0091	0.0034	-0.0057	0.2380
Implementation and impact of individual standards	0.8570	7.0140	6.1570	0.0000
General other	0.0002	0.0032	0.0030	0.0200
TOTAL	1.3030	8.0130	6.7100	0.0000

Panel B – Numerical

Type of disclosure	Pre IFRS	Post IFRS	Diff	P-Value
Factual information	0.0027	0.0000	-0.0027	-
Cost of implementation	0.0016	0.0089	0.0073	0.0000
General impact of implementation	0.0355	0.1616	0.1261	0.0000
Progress to date	0.0000	0.0000	0.0000	-
Operational & strategic decisions taken by management	0.0000	0.0002	0.0002	-
Implementation and impact of individual standards	0.1156	1.6740	1.5584	0.0000
General other	0.0000	0.0026	0.0026	-
TOTAL	0.1555	1.8470	1.6915	0.0000

Notes: This table presents the results of the disaggregation of the IFRS information provided by UK companies by the nature of the information included, for example, whether the disclosure in numerical or narrative in form. This information is based on the percentage of annual report devoted to IFRS-related information by companies across the seven disclosure categories. Panel A presents details the narrative content, while Panel B outlines the numerical content. The mean p-values are based on a 2-sample t-test.

Table D.3 Italy sample – Narrative versus numerical (percentage of annual report devoted to IFRS disclosures)

Panel A – Narrative

Type of disclosure	Pre IFRS	Post IFRS	Diff	P-Value
Factual information	0.4514	2.3100	1.8586	0.0000
Cost of implementation	0.0668	0.0000	-0.0668	-
General impact of implementation	0.1135	0.0115	-0.1020	0.0000
Progress to date	0.2689	0.0050	-0.2639	0.0000
Operational & strategic decisions taken by management	0.0014	0.0000	-0.0014	-
Implementation and impact of individual standards	0.6250	11.1850	10.5600	0.0000
General other	0.0144	0.0374	0.0230	0.2820
TOTAL	1.5410	13.5480	12.0070	0.0000

Panel B – Numerical

Type of disclosure	Pre IFRS	Post IFRS	Diff	
Factual information	0.0000	0.0000	0.0000	-
Cost of implementation	0.0423	0.0000	-0.0423	-
General impact of implementation	0.0236	0.0704	0.0468	0.1830
Progress to date	0.0000	0.0000	0.0000	-
Operational & strategic decisions taken by management	0.0016	0.0000	-0.0016	-
Implementation and impact of individual standards	0.0646	16.1540	16.0894	0.0000
General other	0.0000	0.0219	0.0219	-
TOTAL	0.1321	16.2470	16.1149	0.0000

Notes: This table presents the results of the disaggregation of the IFRS information provided by Italian companies by the nature of the information included, for example, whether the disclosure in numerical or narrative in form. This information is based on the percentage of annual report devoted to IFRS-related information by companies across the seven disclosure categories. Panel A presents details the narrative content, while Panel B outlines the numerical content. The mean p-values are based on a 2-sample t-test.

Table D.4 Ireland sample – Narrative versus numerical (percentage of annual report devoted to IFRS disclosures)

Panel A – Narrative

Type of disclosure	Pre IFRS	Post IFRS	Diff	P-Value
Factual information	0.3930	1.0040	0.6110	0.0040
Cost of implementation	0.0037	0.0005	-0.0032	0.4140
General impact of implementation	0.7290	0.0920	-0.6370	0.7360
Progress to date	0.0698	0.0080	-0.0618	0.0020
Operational & strategic decisions taken by management	0.0000	0.0000	0.0000	-
Implementation and impact of individual standards	2.0400	10.3050	8.2650	0.0000
General other	0.0000	0.0000	0.0000	-
TOTAL	2.5800	11.4090	8.8290	0.0000

Panel B – Numerical

Type of disclosure	Pre IFRS	Post IFRS	Diff	P-Value
Factual information	0.0000	0.0000	0.0000	-
Cost of implementation	0.0012	0.0010	-0.0002	0.8910
General impact of implementation	0.0259	0.2440	0.2181	0.2720
Progress to date	0.0000	0.0000	0.0000	-
Operational & strategic decisions taken by management	0.0000	0.0000	0.0000	-
Implementation and impact of individual standards	0.3490	1.6730	1.3240	0.0180
General other	0.0000	0.0000	0.0000	-
TOTAL	0.3760	1.9180	1.5420	0.0019

Notes: This table presents the results of the disaggregation of the IFRS information provided by Irish companies by the nature of the information included, for example, whether the disclosure in numerical or narrative in form. This information is based on the percentage of annual report devoted to IFRS-related information by companies across the seven disclosure categories. Panel A presents details the narrative content, while Panel B outlines the numerical content. The mean p-values are based on a 2-sample t-test.

Table D.5 Disclosure by standard (percentage of annual report)

Panel A - UK

Standard	Pre IFRS	Post IFRS	Diff
IAS 1	0.0200	0.1580	0.1380
IAS 2	0.0040	0.8790	0.8750
IAS 7	0.0040	0.0960	0.0920
IAS 8	0.0010	0.0010	0.0000
IAS 10	0.0340	0.1330	0.0990
IAS 11	0.0010	0.0170	0.0160
IAS 12	0.0800	0.5900	0.5100
IAS 14	0.0080	0.0920	0.0840
IAS 16	0.0280	0.3760	0.3480
IAS 17	0.0210	0.2350	0.2140
IAS 18	0.0180	0.2710	0.2530
IAS 19	0.1110	0.9360	0.8250
IAS 20	0.0000	0.0130	0.0130
IAS 21	0.0260	0.3480	0.3220
IAS 23	0.0010	0.0350	0.0340
IAS 24	0.0000	0.0520	0.0520
IAS 26	0.0000	0.0000	0.0000
IAS 27	0.0220	0.2300	0.2080
IAS 28	0.0090	0.0550	0.0470
IAS 29	0.0010	0.0010	0.0010
IAS 30	0.0000	0.0000	0.0000
IAS 31	0.0130	0.0630	0.0500
IAS 33	0.0120	0.0400	0.0280
IAS 34	0.0000	0.0000	0.0000
IAS 36	0.0090	0.2480	0.2390
IAS 37	0.0090	0.2040	0.1950
IAS 38	0.0470	0.3670	0.3200
IAS 40	0.0040	0.0470	0.0430
IAS 41	0.0070	0.0090	0.0020
IFRS 1	0.0190	0.1560	0.1370
IFRS 2	0.1200	0.4970	0.3770
IFRS 3	0.0350	0.2440	0.2090
IFRS 4	0.0220	0.1350	0.1130
IFRS 5	0.0540	0.1130	0.0590
IFRS 6	0.0000	0.0180	0.0180
IAS 28/31	0.0070	0.0520	0.0450
IAS 32/39/IFRS 7	0.2180	2.4330	2.2150
Goodwill	0.0500	0.2690	0.2190

Notes: This table presents the results of the breakdown of the IFRS information provided by companies by standard. This information is based on the percentage of annual report devoted to IFRS-related information by companies across the seven disclosure categories. Panel A provides the UK results, while Panel B and C concentrate on the Italian and Irish results respectively. The mean p-values are based on a 2-sample t-test.

Table D.5 Disclosure by standard (percentage of annual report) (cont.)

Panel B - Italy

Standard	Pre IFRS	Post IFRS	Diff
IAS 1	0.0120	0.1720	0.1600
IAS 2	0.0010	0.1190	0.1180
IAS 7	0.0010	0.1800	0.1790
IAS 8	0.0000	0.0030	0.0030
IAS 10	0.0000	0.0000	0.0000
IAS 11	0.0000	0.1140	0.1140
IAS 12	0.0060	1.0680	1.0620
IAS 14	0.0030	2.5050	2.5020
IAS 16	0.0230	0.3270	0.3040
IAS 17	0.0360	0.2500	0.2140
IAS 18	0.0190	0.2040	0.1850
IAS 19	0.0520	1.3310	1.2790
IAS 20	0.0000	0.0490	0.0490
IAS 21	0.0060	0.2610	0.2550
IAS 23	0.0010	0.2040	0.2030
IAS 24	0.0070	0.9600	0.9530
IAS 26	0.0000	0.1420	0.1420
IAS 27	0.0380	0.7740	0.7360
IAS 28	0.0040	0.4320	0.4280
IAS 29	0.0000	0.0010	0.0010
IAS 30	0.0000	0.0000	0.0000
IAS 31	0.0050	0.2540	0.2490
IAS 33	0.0120	0.2570	0.2450
IAS 34	0.0000	0.0000	0.0000
IAS 36	0.0630	0.6970	0.6340
IAS 37	0.0360	0.9380	0.9020
IAS 38	0.0280	0.3210	0.2930
IAS 40	0.0010	0.1480	0.1470
IAS 41	0.0000	0.0000	0.0000
IFRS 1	0.0860	0.3470	0.2610
IFRS 2	0.0230	1.3130	1.29001
IFRS 3	0.0180	0.7150	0.6970
IFRS 4	0.0050	0.6420	0.6370
IFRS 5	0.0370	0.3810	0.3440
IFRS 6	0.0020	0.0210	0.0190
IAS 32/39/IFRS 7	0.1650	12.4190	12.2540

Notes: This table presents the results of the breakdown of the IFRS information provided by companies by standard. This information is based on the percentage of annual report devoted to IFRS-related information by companies across the seven disclosure categories. Panel A provides the UK results, while Panel B and C concentrate on the Italian and Irish results respectively. The mean p-values are based on a 2-sample t-test.

Table D.5 Disclosure by standard (percentage of annual report) (cont.)

Panel C - Ireland

Standard	Pre IFRS	Post IFRS	Diff
IAS 1	0.0420	0.0970	0.0550
IAS 2	0.0090	0.1140	0.1050
IAS 7	0.0000	0.0670	0.0670
IAS 8	0.0000	0.0000	0.0000
IAS 10	0.0420	0.1480	0.1060
IAS 11	0.0000	0.0260	0.0260
IAS 12	0.2530	0.6310	0.3780
IAS 14	0.0430	0.0810	0.0380
IAS 16	0.0550	0.5210	0.4660
IAS 17	0.0440	0.1750	0.1310
IAS 18	0.0310	0.6080	0.5770
IAS 19	0.2780	1.0200	0.7420
IAS 20	0.0070	0.0640	0.0570
IAS 21	0.0930	0.5600	0.4670
IAS 23	0.0000	0.0360	0.0360
IAS 24	0.0000	0.1520	0.1520
IAS 26	0.0000	0.0000	0.0000
IAS 27	0.0610	0.2800	0.2190
IAS 28	0.0160	0.1490	0.1330
IAS 29	0.0000	0.0000	0.0000
IAS 30	0.0000	0.0000	0.0000
IAS 31	0.0040	0.0920	0.0880
IAS 33	0.0660	0.0260	-0.0400
IAS 34	0.0000	0.0000	0.0000
IAS 36	0.0340	0.2280	0.1940
IAS 37	0.0000	0.2370	0.2370
IAS 38	0.1390	0.3880	0.2490
IAS 40	0.0000	0.0120	0.0120
IAS 41	0.0000	0.0000	0.0000
IFRS 1	0.0310	0.1730	0.1420
IFRS 2	0.1370	0.6010	0.4640
IFRS 3	0.1820	0.2730	0.0910
IFRS 4	0.0090	0.2140	0.2050
IFRS 5	0.0000	0.1500	0.1500
IFRS 6	0.0000	0.0080	0.0080
IAS 28/31	0.0740	0.1180	0.0440
IAS 32/39/IFRS 7	0.6640	4.2300	3.5660
Goodwill	0.0730	0.4580	0.3850

Notes: This table presents the results of the breakdown of the IFRS information provided by companies by standard. This information is based on the percentage of annual report devoted to IFRS-related information by companies across the seven disclosure categories. Panel A provides the UK results, while Panel B and C concentrate on the Italian and Irish results respectively. The mean p-values are based on a 2-sample t-test.

APPENDIX E

DETAILED RESPONSES TO INTERVIEW QUESTIONS BY COUNTRY AND STAKEHOLDER GROUP

Table E1 Irish preparers' and auditor's experiences of IFRS implementation

	Irish Preparers				Irish Auditor
	IR1P	IR2P	IR3P	IR4P	IR5A
IFRS consultation during and prior to IFRS implementation					
Wide consultation?	Yes	No	Yes	Yes	Yes
With competitors?	Yes	-	Yes	Yes	Yes
With regulators/auditors	Yes	No	Yes	Yes	-
Much time at AGM?	No	No	No	No	-
Disclosure					
Does poor disclosure send a bad signal to the market?	No	-	-	Yes	No
Good disclosure advantageous?	No	No	Yes	No	Yes
Capital structure impacted?	-	-	No	No	-
Costs- Impact on:					
Disclosure of strategic information?	No	No	No	No	Yes
Investment, dividend, finance decisions?	Yes	No	Yes	No	-
Taxation?	Yes	No	Yes	No	Yes
Share price?	No	No	No	No	No
Have costs been passed to shareholders?	Yes	No	No	No	-
Benefits					
Lower cost of capital?	No	No	No	No	-
Better assessment of management performance?	Yes	No	Yes	No	-
Improved predictive ability for users?	-	No	No	No	Yes
Better company performance analysis by investors?	No	No	No	No	-
Better informed decisions for users?	Yes	Yes	No	-	No
Overall opinion					
Are new IFRS formats more useful to users?	No	No	-	-	Yes
Do the benefits of IFRS outweigh the costs?	No	No	Unsure	No	Unsure

* Preparers and auditors were asked whether IFRS would affect company investment decisions.

Table E2 Italian preparers', auditors', regulators' and users' experiences of IFRS implementation

	Italian preparers			
	IT1P	IT2P	IT3P	IT4P
IFRS consultation during and prior to IFRS implementation				
Wide consultation?	Yes	Yes	Yes	Yes
With competitors and benchmarking?	Yes	No	No	Yes
With regulators/auditors	Yes	Yes	Yes	Yes
Much time at AGM?	No	No	No	Yes
Disclosure				
Does poor disclosure send a bad signal to the market?	Yes	Yes	Yes	Yes
Good disclosure advantageous to reputation?	Yes	Yes	Yes	Yes
Capital structure impacted?	No	No	No	No
Costs - Impact on:				
Disclosure of strategic information?	No	No	No	No
Investment, dividend, finance decisions? *	No	Yes	Yes	Yes
Taxation?	No	No	Yes	Yes
Share price?	No	No	No	No
Have costs been passed to shareholders?	No	No	No	No
Benefits				
Lower cost of capital?	No	No	No	No
Better assessment of management performance?	No	-	No	Yes
Improved predictive ability for users?	Yes	Yes	Yes	No
Better company performance analysis by investors?	Yes	Yes	Yes	Yes
Better informed decisions for users?	Yes	No	Yes	Yes
Overall opinion				
Are new IFRS formats more useful to users?	Yes	Yes	Yes	Yes
Do the benefits of IFRS outweigh the costs?	Unsure	No	No	No

* Preparers and auditors were asked whether IFRS would affect company investment decisions while users were asked whether their own investment decisions had changed.

Table E2 Italian preparers', auditors', regulators' and users' experiences of IFRS implementation (cont.)

	Italian auditor	Italian regulator	Italian users	
	IT5A	IT8R	IT6U	IT7U
IFRS consultation during and prior to IFRS implementation				
Wide consultation?	Yes	-	Yes	Yes
With competitors and benchmarking?	-	-	No	Yes
With regulators/auditors	-	-	No	Yes
Much time at AGM?	-	No	No	No
Disclosure				
Does poor disclosure send a bad signal to the market?	Yes	Yes	Yes	Yes
Good disclosure advantageous to reputation?	Yes	Yes	Yes	Yes
Capital structure impacted?	-	No	No	No
Costs - Impact on:				
Disclosure of strategic information?	Yes	No	No	No
Investment, dividend, finance decisions? *	-	-	No	Unsure
Taxation?	Yes	Yes	No	No
Share price?	No	No	No	No
Have costs been passed to shareholders?	-	-	No	No
Benefits				
Lower cost of capital?	No	Yes	Yes	Yes
Better assessment of management performance?	-	Yes	No	Yes
Improved predictive ability for users?	Yes	Yes	Yes	Yes
Better company performance analysis by investors?	Yes	-	-	-
Better informed decisions for users?	Yes	Yes	Yes	Yes
Overall opinion				
Are new IFRS formats more useful to users?	Yes	Yes	Yes	Yes
Do the benefits of IFRS outweigh the costs?	No	No	-	No

* Preparers and auditors were asked whether IFRS would affect company investment decisions while users were asked whether their own investment decisions had changed.

Table E3 UK auditors', regulators' and account users' experiences of IFRS implementation

	UK auditors			
	UK1A	UK2A	UK3A	UK4A
IFRS consultation during and prior to IFRS implementation				
Wide consultation?	Yes	Yes	Yes	Yes
With competitors and benchmarking?	Yes	Yes	Yes	Yes
With regulators/auditors	-	-	No	Yes
Much time at AGM?	No	No	No	Unsure
Disclosure				
Does poor disclosure send a bad signal to the market?	-	-	No	Yes
Good disclosure advantageous to reputation?	-	Yes	Unsure	Yes
Capital structure impacted?	-	No	No	Yes
Costs - Impact on:				
Disclosure of strategic information?	Yes	Yes	Yes	-
Investment, dividend, finance decisions? *	No	-	No	Yes
Taxation?	No	No	-	Yes
Share price?	-	No	No	No
Have costs been passed to shareholders?	Yes	Yes	Yes	Yes
Benefits				
Lower cost of capital?	-	Yes	No	No
Better assessment of management performance?	Yes	-	-	Yes
Improved predictive ability for users?	-	No	No	No
Better company performance analysis by investors?	-	No	No	No
Better informed decisions for users?	-	-	-	-
Overall opinion				
Are new IFRS formats more useful to users?	No	No	No	No
Do the benefits of IFRS outweigh the costs?	No	No	No	Unsure

* Auditors were asked whether IFRS would affect company investment decisions while users were asked whether their own investment decisions had changed due to the new standards.

Table E3 UK auditors', regulators' and account users' experiences of IFRS implementation (cont.)

	UK regulators		
	UK1R	UK2R	UK3R
IFRS consultation during and prior to IFRS implementation			
Wide consultation?	Yes	Yes	Yes
With competitors and benchmarking?	Yes	Yes	Yes
With regulators/auditors	-	-	-
Much time at AGM?	No	Unsure	-
Disclosure			
Does poor disclosure send a bad signal to the market?	Unsure	-	Yes
Good disclosure advantageous to reputation?	Yes	Yes	Yes
Capital structure impacted?	-	Unsure	No
Costs - Impact on:			
Disclosure of strategic information?	Yes	Yes	Yes
Investment, dividend, finance decisions? *	-	-	-
Taxation?	No	Unsure	Unsure
Share price?	-	Unsure	-
Have costs been passed to shareholders?	-	-	-
Benefits			
Lower cost of capital?	Unsure	Yes	Yes
Better assessment of management performance?	Yes	Unsure	-
Improved predictive ability for users?	-	Unsure	-
Better company performance analysis by investors?	-	-	-
Better informed decisions for users?	-	Yes	-
Overall opinion			
Are new IFRS formats more useful to users?	-	-	-
Do the benefits of IFRS outweigh the costs?	-	Unsure	-

* Auditors were asked whether IFRS would affect company investment decisions while users were asked whether their own investment decisions had changed due to the new standards.

Table E3 UK auditors', regulators' and account users' experiences of IFRS implementation (cont.)

	UK users		
	UK1U	UK2U	UK3U
IFRS consultation during and prior to IFRS implementation			
Wide consultation?	Yes	No	No
With competitors and benchmarking?	Yes	No	No
With regulators/auditors	Yes	-	-
Much time at AGM?	Unsure	Unsure	Unsure
Disclosure			
Does poor disclosure send a bad signal to the market?	Yes	-	-
Good disclosure advantageous to reputation?	Yes	No	-
Capital structure impacted?	No	No	-
Costs - Impact on:			
Disclosure of strategic information?	Yes	Yes	-
Investment, dividend, finance decisions? *	No	No	No
Taxation?	No	No	-
Share price?	No	-	-
Have costs been passed to shareholders?	-	Yes	-
Benefits			
Lower cost of capital?	Yes	-	-
Better assessment of management performance?	No	Unsure	-
Improved predictive ability for users?	-	No	-
Better company performance analysis by investors?	-	-	
Better informed decisions for users?	No	-	-
Overall opinion			
Are new IFRS formats more useful to users?	No	Yes	No
Do the benefits of IFRS outweigh the costs?	Unsure	No	-

* Auditors were asked whether IFRS would affect company investment decisions while users were asked whether their own investment decisions had changed due to the new standards.

Table E4 UK preparers' experiences of IFRS implementation

	UK preparers				
	UK1P	UK2P	UK3P	UK4P	UK5P
IFRS consultation during and prior to IFRS implementation					
Wide consultation?	Yes	Yes	Yes	Yes	Yes
With competitors and benchmarking?	-	Yes	Yes	Yes	Yes
With regulators/auditors	-	-	-	-	-
Much time at AGM?	No	No	No	No	No
Disclosure					
Poor disclosure= bad signal	Yes	Yes	No	-	-
Good disclosure advantageous to reputation?	-	-	Unsure	Yes	Yes
Capital structure impacted?	No	No	-	-	-
Costs - Impact on:					
Disclosure of strategic information?	Yes	Yes	Yes	No	No
Investment, dividend, finance decisions? *	No	No	No	No	No
Taxation?	No	No	No	-	-
Share price?	-	No	No	Yes	Yes
Have costs been passed to shareholders?	-	Yes	Yes	Yes	Yes
Benefits					
Lower cost of capital?	No	-	No	Yes	Yes
Better assessment of management performance?	No	Yes	No	Yes	Yes
Improved predictive ability for users?	-	No	-	Yes	Yes
Better company performance analysis by investors?	No	No	-	Yes	Yes
Better informed decisions for users?	-	-	-	Yes	Yes
Overall opinion					
Are new IFRS formats more useful to users?	-	Yes	No	No	No
Do the benefits of IFRS outweigh the costs?	No	No	No	No	No

* Preparers and auditors were asked whether IFRS would affect company investment decisions while users were asked whether their own investment decisions would change as a result of the new standards.

Table E4 UK accounts preparers' experiences of IFRS implementation (cont.)

	UK preparers			
	UK6P	UK7P	UK8P	UK9P
IFRS consultation during and prior to IFRS implementation				
Wide consultation?	Yes	Yes	Yes	Yes
With competitors and benchmarking?	Yes	Yes	Yes	Yes
With regulators/auditors	Yes	-	-	-
Much time at AGM?	No	No	No	No
Disclosure				
Poor disclosure= bad signal	-	Yes	-	-
Good disclosure advantageous to reputation?	-	Yes	No	-
Capital structure impacted?	-	No	Yes	No
Costs - Impact on:				
Disclosure of strategic information?	No	-	Yes	Yes
Investment, dividend, finance decisions? *	No	No	Yes	-
Taxation?	No	No	-	No
Share price?	No	No	-	-
Have costs been passed to shareholders?	-	Yes	Yes	Unsure
Benefits				
Lower cost of capital?	No	No	No	-
Better assessment of management performance?	No	No	-	-
Improved predictive ability for users?	-	Unsure	-	-
Better company performance analysis by investors?	No	-	-	-
Better informed decisions for users?	-	-	Yes	-
Overall opinion				
Are new IFRS formats more useful to users?	-	No	Yes	No
Do the benefits of IFRS outweigh the costs?	No	No	-	No

* Preparers and auditors were asked whether IFRS would affect company investment decisions while users were asked whether their own investment decisions would change as a result of the new standards.

APPENDIX F

LIST OF INTERNATIONAL FINANCIAL REPORTING STANDARDS

International Financial Reporting Standards (IFRSs)

IFRS 1	First-time Adoption of International Financial Reporting Standards
IFRS 2	Share-based Payment
IFRS 3	Business Combinations
IFRS 4	Insurance Contracts
IFRS 5	Non-current Assets Held for Sale and Discontinued Operations
IFRS 6	Exploration for and evaluation of Mineral Resources
IFRS 7	Financial Instruments: Disclosures (**effective for accounting periods beginning on or after 1 January 2007, earlier application is encouraged**)
IFRS 8	Operating Segments (**effective for accounting periods beginning on or after 1 January 2009, earlier application is permitted**)

International Accounting Standards (IASs)

IAS 1	Presentation of Financial Statements
IAS 2	Inventories
IAS 7	Cash Flow Statements
IAS 8	Accounting Policies, Changes in Accounting Estimates and Errors
IAS 10	Events After the Balance Sheet Date
IAS 11	Construction Contracts
IAS 12	Income Taxes
IAS 14	Segment Reporting (**withdrawn and replaced by IFRS 8 for accounting periods beginning on or after 1 January 2009**)
IAS 16	Property, Plant and Equipment
IAS 17	Leases

IAS 18	Revenue
IAS 19	Employee Benefits
IAS 20	Accounting for Government Grants and Disclosure of Government Assistance
IAS 21	The Effects of Changes in Foreign Exchange Rates
IAS 23	Borrowing Costs
IAS 24	Related Party Disclosures
IAS 26	Accounting and Reporting by Retirement Benefit Plans
IAS 27	Consolidated and Separate Financial Statements
IAS 28	Investments in Associates
IAS 29	Financial Reporting in Hyperinflationary Economies
IAS 30	Disclosures in the Financial Statements of Banks and Similar Financial Institutions (**withdrawn and replaced by IFRS 7 for accounting periods beginning on or after 1 January 2007**)
IAS 31	Interests in Joint Ventures
IAS 32	Financial Instruments: Presentation
IAS 33	Earnings per Share
IAS 34	Interim Financial Reporting
IAS 36	Impairment of Assets
IAS 37	Provisions, Contingent Liabilities and Contingent Assets
IAS 38	Intangible Assets
IAS 39	Financial Instruments: Recognition and Measurement
IAS 40	Investment Property
IAS 41	Agriculture

The above list is based on standards in force for periods beginning on or after 1st January 2005. Standards effective for later periods are also highlighted as well as those which have subsequently been withdrawn.

About the Authors

Theresa Dunne is a Lecturer in the School of Accounting & Finance at the University of Dundee. She was awarded her PhD on the implications of derivatives accounting and reporting for accountability and corporate governance from the same university. Dr. Dunne has published in a wide range of academic and professional journals on areas such as accountability, financial reporting, accounting standard setting, charity accounting and governance, international accounting, Internet reporting, treasury practice and control and corporate governance and sits on the Editorial Board of the Journal of International Accounting, Auditing and Taxation.

Suzanne Fifield is a Senior Lecturer in Finance at the University of Dundee. Her research interests are primarily in the broad area of international finance, with a particular emphasis on emerging stock markets. Specific areas of research include: stock market efficiency, international portfolio diversification, the performance of technical trading rules, Central and Eastern European emerging stock markets, African equity markets and the Chinese stock market. She has published numerous refereed articles in these areas.

Gary Finningham is a research student at the University of Dundee. His undergraduate degree was in Accountancy and his postgraduate studies have focused on the implementation of IFRS within the UK. In particular, he has examined the impact of IFRS on the published financial statements of UK companies.

Alison Fox trained with Ernst and Young and became ACCA qualified in 1993. After a short time in industry she began her academic career in 1995 and now teaches financial accounting, taxation and business law to under-graduate students at the University of Dundee. She is also currently studying for a PhD entitled 'An Investigation of the Corporate Governance and Accountability of Pension Schemes'. Other research interests include financial accounting (specifically Deferred Taxation and the implementation of IFRS) and accounting education.

Gwen Hannah is a Lecturer in the School of Accounting & Finance at the University of Dundee. She worked in banking before commencing her accounting education and an examination of accountability in primary health care gained her a PhD in 2003. Her research interests include not for profit and public sector accountability and the role of trust in stakeholder relationships.

Christine Helliar is Professor of Treasury Management at the University of Dundee. She trained as a Chartered Accountant at Ernst & Young in London before moving into Investment Banking, where she worked at Morgan Stanley, HSBC Group and Citigroup. She then moved into academia and her research interests are financial reporting, corporate governance, treasury management, auditing and accounting education.

David M. Power is Professor of Business Finance at the University of Dundee. He currently lectures on Financial Management, Financial Statement Analysis and Security Analysis & Portfolio Management. His research interests include share valuation approaches and stock market performance in emerging as well as developed countries. In addition, his published work has focussed on how companies communicate with financial markets. He is on a number of editorial boards and has refereed for several journals.

Monica Veneziani is full time Assistant Professor of Accounting at the University of Brescia, Italy. She is currently teaching Accounting and Financial Statement Analysis at both postgraduate and masters level at the University. Her research interests are financial reporting, financial analysis, international accounting standards and financial communication.